California
Public School Library Act

P9-BBP-607

DISCARD

DISCARD

The Age of Exploration

Titles in the World History Series

The Age of Augustus
The Age of Exploration
The Age of Feudalism
The Age of Napoleon
The Age of Pericles
The Alamo
America in the 1960s
The American Frontier
The American Revolution
Ancient Greece
The Ancient Near East
Architecture
Aztec Civilization
The Battle of the
    Little Bighorn
The Black Death
The Byzantine Empire
Caesar's Conquest of Gaul
The California Gold Rush
The Chinese Cultural
    Revolution
The Civil Rights Movement
The Collapse of the
    Roman Republic
The Conquest of Mexico
The Crimean War
The Crusades
The Cuban Missile Crisis
The Cuban Revolution
The Early Middle Ages
Egypt of the Pharaohs
Elizabethan England
The End of the Cold War
The Enlightenment
The French and Indian War
The French Revolution
The Glorious Revolution
The Great Depression
Greek and Roman
    Mythology
Greek and Roman Science

Greek and Roman Sport
Greek and Roman Theater
The History of Slavery
Hitler's Reich
The Hundred Years' War
The Industrial Revolution
The Inquisition
The Italian Renaissance
The Late Middle Ages
The Lewis and Clark
    Expedition
The Mexican Revolution
The Mexican War of
    Independence
Modern Japan
The Mongol Empire
The Persian Empire
Prohibition
The Punic Wars
The Reformation
The Relocation of the
    North American Indian
The Renaissance
The Roaring Twenties
The Roman Empire
The Roman Republic
Roosevelt and the New Deal
The Russian Revolution
Russia of the Tsars
The Scientific Revolution
The Spread of Islam
The Stone Age
The Titanic
Traditional Africa
Traditional Japan
The Travels of Marco Polo
Twentieth Century Science
The Wars of the Roses
The Watts Riot
Women's Suffrage

INDEPENDENCE HIGH SCHOOL LIBRARY

The Age of Exploration

by
Sarah Flowers

Lucent Books, P.O. Box 289011, San Diego, CA 92198-9011

For my father,
whose sense of exploration and love of history
enlivened our family vacations.

Library of Congress Cataloging-in-Publication Data

Flowers, Sarah, 1952–
    The age of exploration / by Sarah Flowers.
        p. cm. — (World history series)
    Includes bibliographical references and index.
    Summary: Discusses the discoveries of several notable
explorers active between 1492 and 1522, including
Columbus, Da Gama, Drake, and Magellan.
    ISBN 1-56006-258-4 (lib. : alk. paper)
    1. Discoveries in geography—History—15th century—
Juvenile literature.   2. Discoveries in geography—History—
16th century—Juvenile literature.   3. Explorers—Biography—
Juvenile literature.   [1. Discoveries in geography.   2. Explorers.]   I. Title.   II. Series.
G82.F56   1999
910'.9'024—dc21   98-27772
                                     CIP
                                     AC

Copyright 1999 by Lucent Books, Inc., P.O. Box 289011,
San Diego, California 92198-9011

Printed in the U.S.A.

No part of this book may be reproduced or used in any other
form or by any other means, electrical, mechanical, or otherwise, including, but not limited to, photocopy, recording, or
any information storage and retrieval system, without prior written permission from the publisher.

Contents

Foreword

Each year on the first day of school, nearly every history teacher faces the task of explaining why his or her students should study history. One logical answer to this question is that exploring what happened in our past explains how the things we often take for granted—our customs, ideas, and institutions—came to be. As statesman and historian Winston Churchill put it, "Every nation or group of nations has its own tale to tell. Knowledge of the trials and struggles is necessary to all who would comprehend the problems, perils, challenges, and opportunities which confront us today." Thus, a study of history puts modern ideas and institutions in perspective. For example, though the founders of the United States were talented and creative thinkers, they clearly did not invent the concept of democracy. Instead, they adapted some democratic ideas that had originated in ancient Greece and with which the Romans, the British, and others had experimented. An exploration of these cultures, then, reveals their very real connection to us through institutions that continue to shape our daily lives.

Another reason often given for studying history is the idea that lessons exist in the past from which contemporary societies can benefit and learn. This idea, although controversial, has always been an intriguing one for historians. Those who agree that society can benefit from the past often quote philosopher George Santayana's famous statement, "Those who cannot remember the past are condemned to repeat it." Historians who subscribe to Santayana's philosophy believe that, for example, studying the events that led up to the major world wars or other significant historical events would allow society to chart a different and more favorable course in the future.

Just as difficult as convincing students to realize the importance of studying history is the search for useful and interesting supplementary materials that present historical events in a context that can be easily understood. The volumes in Lucent Books' World History Series attempt to present a broad, balanced, and penetrating view of the march of history. Ancient Egypt's important wars and rulers, for example, are presented against the rich and colorful backdrop of Egyptian religious, social, and cultural developments. The series engages the reader by enhancing historical events with these cultural contexts. For example, in *Ancient Greece*, the text covers the role of women in that society. Slavery is discussed in *The Roman Empire*, as well as how slaves earned their freedom. The numerous and varied aspects of everyday life in these and other societies are explored in each volume of the series. Additionally, the series covers the major political, cultural, and philosophical ideas as the torch of civilization is passed from ancient Mesopotamia and Egypt, through Greece, Rome, Medieval Europe, and other world cultures, to the modern day.

The material in the series is formatted in a thorough, precise, and organized manner. Each volume offers the reader a comprehensive and clearly written overview of an important historical event or period. The topic under discussion is placed in a broad historical context. For example, *The Italian Renaissance* begins with a discussion of the High Middle Ages and the loss of central control that allowed certain Italian cities to develop artistically. The book ends by looking forward to the Reformation and interpreting the societal changes that grew out of the Renaissance. Thus, students are not only involved in an historical era, but also enveloped by the events leading up to that era and the events following it.

One important and unique feature in the World History Series is the primary and secondary source quotations that richly supplement each volume. These quotes are useful in a number of ways. First, they allow students access to sources they would not normally be exposed to because of the difficulty and obscurity of the original source. The quotations range from interesting anecdotes to farsighted cultural perspectives and are drawn from historical witnesses both past and present. Second, the quotes demonstrate how and where historians themselves derive their information on the past as they strive to reach a consensus on historical events. Lastly, all of the quotes are footnoted, familiarizing students with the citation process and allowing them to verify quotes and/or look up the original source if the quote piques their interest.

Finally, the books in the World History Series provide a detailed launching point for further research. Each book contains a bibliography specifically geared toward student research. A second, annotated bibliography introduces students to all the sources the author consulted when compiling the book. A chronology of important dates gives students an overview, at a glance, of the topic covered. Where applicable, a glossary of terms is included.

In short, the series is designed not only to acquaint readers with the basics of history, but also to make them aware that their lives are a part of an ongoing human saga. Perhaps they will then come to the same realization as famed historian Arnold Toynbee. In his monumental work, *A Study of History*, he wrote about becoming aware of history flowing through him in a mighty current, and of his own life "welling like a wave in the flow of this vast tide."

Important Dates in the Age of Exploration

1410	1420	1430	1440	1450	1460	1470	1480	1490

1418

Henry the Navigator builds his observatory at Sagres.

1434

Gil Eannes rounds Cape Bojador.

1441

Slave trade begins on the African coast.

1445

Dinas Dias discovers Cape Verde.

1451

Columbus born.

1460

Henry the Navigator dies.

1480

Magellan born.

1484

Portuguese king, João II, refuses to finance Columbus.

1488

Bartolomeu Dias rounds Cape of Good Hope.

1492

Columbus's first voyage.

1494

Treaty of Tordesillas divides the world between Spain and Portugal.

1497

The Cabots reach North America.

1498

Vasco da Gama discovers a sea route to India.

1499

Vespucci and Ojeda leave Spain for South America.

1500

Cabral sights Brazil.

1502

Columbus's fourth (and last) voyage.

1506

Columbus dies.

1507

Martin Waldseemüller's world map labels the southern continent "America."

1500	1510	1520	1530	1540	1550	1560	1570	1580

1511

Albuquerque occupies Goa, giving the Portuguese a base in the East.

1513

Balboa crosses Isthmus of Panama; Ponce de León begins to explore the coast of Florida; Portuguese sail to Canton, China, and the Moluccas.

1515

Solis reaches mouth of Rio de la Plata.

1519

Cortés enters Tenochtitlán, the first step in the conquest of the Aztec Empire; Magellan leaves Spain on circumnavigation voyage.

1520

Magellan passes through strait.

1521

Magellan dies, Juan Sebastián del Cano continues the voyage; Cortés completes the conquest of the Aztecs.

1522

del Cano and eighteen survivors arrive in Spain after circumnavigating the globe.

1524

Verrazano discovers New York Bay and Hudson River.

1532

Pizarro conquers the Inca Empire.

1534

Cartier visits Prince Edward Island.

1539

de Soto explores Florida and points west; Ulloa explores the Gulf of California.

1540–1542

Coronado's expedition into the mainland of North America.

1542

Cabrillo explores San Diego Harbor, sails the California coast to Drake's Bay.

1577–1580

Drake's circumnavigation.

A New View of the World

In one generation, from 1492 to 1522, the world changed completely and forever. A few hundred curious, daring, imaginative, reckless, and determined men redrew the map of the world and connected almost all its parts. They changed the world's eating habits. They caused the downfall of civilizations and contributed to the rise of others. They pushed forward the sciences of mapmaking and navigation, and they put their European stamp on two entire continents.

Exploration and discovery go on all the time, even today. People always seem to be driven to learn more about the universe they live in. But the fifteenth and sixteenth centuries are known as the age of exploration because of the dramatic burst of activity that resulted in nearly quadrupling the known extent of the world.

In 1418 Prince Henry of Portugal set up a headquarters from which he conceived, planned, and organized expeditions to previously unknown parts of the world. Although he never left home, he became known as Henry the Navigator, and his activities signal the beginning of the age of exploration. One hundred sixty-two years later, in 1580, an English captain named Francis Drake returned to his homeland from a three-year voyage during which he circumnavigated the globe and explored the west coasts of both North and South America.

Between those years, and centering on the period from 1492 to 1522, came the burst of European exploration and discovery that still captures the imagination. Small groups of sailors set out in wooden

Prince Henry of Portugal organized expeditions to uncharted parts of the world in the early fifteenth century. His efforts signaled the beginning of the age of exploration and earned him the name Henry the Navigator.

A drawing depicts the departure of Columbus and his fleet of ships en route to the New World. The brave sailors who set out on such expeditions often had very little idea of what to expect on their adventure.

ships that seem startlingly small and primitive by today's standards. They often had only the vaguest ideas of what they would find, and sometimes they were very wrong in their expectations. They went for various reasons. Common sailors often went simply because it was a job, or because they felt allegiance to a particular captain. Captains and expedition leaders went because they were promised a share of the anticipated profits—gold or spices, chiefly. Financial backers such as merchants and kings paid for voyages because they expected to gain something: land, power, money, future trade opportunities, or converts to their religion. None were immune to the possibilities of glory: fame and honor.

Collectively, the participants in this great adventure learned that navigable seas connect all the world's landmasses and that it is possible to sail to any of these continents and return home. Although Australia and Antarctica had not yet been explored, their presences were suspected, and it was only a matter of time before they joined the map.

Maps drawn in Europe in the fourteenth century show a medieval worldview. The Mediterranean (*medi* = middle; *terranean* = of the land or world) was indeed the center of the world. Parts of Asia, Africa, and Europe were known and mapped, but south of the equator was Terra Incognita, the unknown world, and the Atlantic was shown as Mare Oceanum, the vast "Ocean Sea" that would presumably lead to China—always assuming one didn't sail into some abyss first. Between the ninth and the fourteenth centuries, the Norse had settled Greenland and explored the North American coast as far south as New England, but the settlements died out and no knowledge of the coastline survived to show up on maps available to the rest of Europe. By the 1520s, though, maps of the world are recognizably the world we know today; and by the 1580s, when Drake returned to England, they were even closer to reality.

That it was western Europeans who accomplished these feats of discovery and exploration had lasting effects on the political history of the world. They brought their languages, their customs, and their religion to whole continents, often virtually stamping out the ancient cultures they had replaced. They connected the Americas to Europe with ties so strong that they still hold more than five hundred years later. They expanded the economy of the world, and especially of Europe, by creating new markets for trade goods as well as new trade routes. They paved the way for European expansion and colonization. They helped European countries take a major step on the road to transforming themselves from inward-looking medieval lands to outward-looking modern countries.

1 Terra Incognita: The Unknown World

When the great age of exploration began in the 1400s, those doing the exploring were not setting out completely into the unknown. They based their journeys on three things. First, there was what they knew of the world, from their own experience and from the reports of others. Second, there was what they thought they knew, based on hundreds of years of stories and tales. Third, there was what scholars and teachers told them should be true, based on systematic attempts to explain the world around them in terms of the scientific knowledge of the day. Some of what they knew or guessed was true, but much was wildly exaggerated, mistakenly calculated, or just plain made up.

Theory: The Greeks

The ancient Greeks considered geography to be an important science, and they devoted a lot of attention to it. They had a very clear picture of the world around the Mediterranean and Black Seas, and some knowledge of Persia and the lands around the Caspian Sea. One or two bold explorers had sailed out of the Mediterranean and north along the coasts of present-day Portugal, France, and Britain, and even farther north. A Greek named Pytheas, who lived during the time of Alexander the Great in the fourth century B.C., journeyed north to the land he called Thule, where the sun never set. Thule was probably Iceland or Norway. The conquests of Alexander the Great expanded the body of knowledge of the world. Alexander and his troops crossed the Indus River and traveled through Afghanistan, farther into Asia than any Europeans had been known to go before.

The ancient Greeks accepted the idea of the earth as a sphere. The great philosopher Aristotle based this knowledge on what he called "the evidence of our senses."[1] He noted that "only a sphere could throw a circular shadow on the Moon during an eclipse."[2] In the third century B.C., a young mathematician named Eratosthenes computed the circumference of the earth, coming very close to the correct value.

Eratosthenes was the second librarian of the great library at Alexandria, at that time the repository of much of the world's knowledge. He used basic math and some sound observations to determine the earth's circumference. First, he heard from travelers that at noon on the summer solstice (June 21), the sun shone in a direct vertical line into a well in

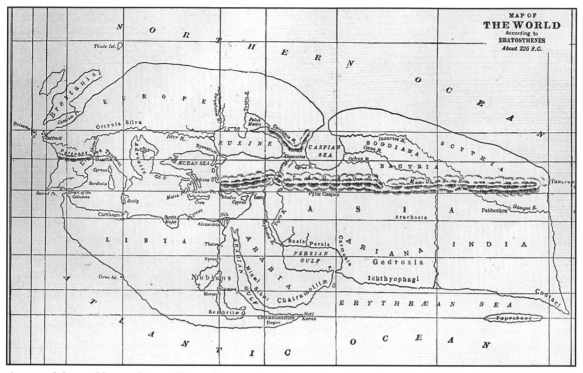

A map of the world according to Eratosthenes, a third-century B.C. *mathematician who used basic math and observations of the sun's patterns to compute the circumference of the earth, and came amazingly close to the accurate value.*

Aswân, a city south of Alexandria. He calculated that Aswân was five hundred miles south of Alexandria, where he lived, and he knew that the sun was never directly overhead in Alexandria. By measuring the shadow of a tower in Alexandria on June 21 at noon, he used trigonometry to determine that the angle created by the sun's rays falling on the top of the tower was about 7°. After equating 7° with 500 miles, the distance between Aswân and Alexandria, Eratosthenes used arithmetic to calculate that each degree was about 71 miles in length. Since the Alexandrians followed Aristotle in believing that the world was round, they normally represented the planet as a circle, of 360°. Thus it was simple enough for Eratosthenes to arrive at

25,560 miles, or 71 × 360° as the total circumference of the earth. These figures are very close to those recognized today: 24,902 miles for the earth's circumference at the equator and about 69 miles for each degree of latitude.

However, Eratosthenes' calculation was not widely accepted, mainly because other geographers contested his calculation for the length of a mile and the distance between Aswân and Alexandria. Not long after, another Greek named Posidonius concluded that the earth's circumference was in fact 18,000 miles, and many of the later geographers, including the great Ptolemy, accepted this figure. Ptolemy was a Greek Egyptian who lived in the second century. He is known for two great works.

The first is *Astronomy*, in which he describes the solar system, with Earth at the center and Mercury, Venus, Mars, Jupiter, Saturn, the Sun, and the Moon revolving around it. The second is *Geography*, in which he attempted to list the latitude and longitude of every known location in the world. As it happened, many of his calculations were wildly wrong, both because he was relying on guesswork and travelers' tales and because his math was based on the inaccurate belief that the earth was 18,000 miles in circumference and that the distance of a degree was 50 miles. But his work had a tremendous effect on everyone

Because Eratosthenes knew the distance between Alexandria and Aswân was 500 miles, he multiplied 50 times 500 and arrived at a figure of 25,000 miles, which is within 1 percent of the actual figure as determined by modern science.

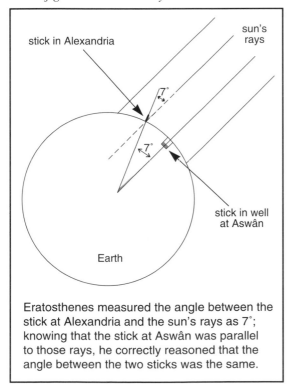

stick in Alexandria

sun's rays

7°

7°

stick in well at Aswân

Earth

Eratosthenes measured the angle between the stick at Alexandria and the sun's rays as 7°; knowing that the stick at Aswân was parallel to those rays, he correctly reasoned that the angle between the two sticks was the same.

for over a thousand years. Columbus relied on Ptolemy's *Geography* when he began to plan his first voyage.

Myth: Romance and Fairy Tales

Stories about the wonders to be found in other parts of the world have existed from the earliest times. In the fifteenth century, people relied on sources that included the classical authors, the Bible, tales brought to Europe by the Muslims, and legends created during the Middle Ages, which were drawing to a close. Most of the tales emphasized the wealth and wonders to be found in distant lands. The Orient "held a particular charm for both classical and medieval men, being associated in their minds with fantastic wealth, natural wonders, and magic."[3] As late as the sixteenth century, explorers were searching for such fabled lands as the Land of Ophir, supposed site of King Solomon's gold and jewels, the River of Gold (El Dorado), and the lost continent of Atlantis.

In about 1410, Cardinal Pierre d'Ailly wrote a geography book called *Imago Mundi*, or *Image of the World*. It was based on the Bible, on Aristotle, and on other theorists' works, but did not incorporate travelers' tales. Among other things, d'Ailly described a massive Asian continent, extending more than halfway around the earth's circumference. The book was a favorite of Columbus, who read it many times and wrote extensive notes in the margins of his copy, which still exists.

The desires to find fabled lands of gold and riches were furthered by the popularity of travelers' tales. In 1145 a bishop named

Otto von Freising recorded that he met a Syrian bishop in Italy who told of a great and powerful Christian king named John "dwelling in the Far East beyond Persia." This king, soon known all over Europe as Prester John, was variously rumored to live in Asia, India, and Africa. In 1170 a letter supposedly from Prester John to various European leaders circulated widely. No one knows who actually wrote it, but it amazed and entertained the people who read it. Among other things,

> it tells how the priest-king was superior in wealth and power to all the other monarchs of the world. . . . His lands were four months' journey across and comprised seventy-two provinces, each of which was ruled by a king. Within

the realm were the lands of the Amazons and the Brahmins, the shrine of St. Thomas the Apostle, the Fountain of Youth, and rivers that ran gold and silver and jewels. Of Prester John himself, it was written that he was descended from the race of the Three Wise Men.[4]

In the fourteenth century another great work of fiction took Europe by storm: *The Travels of Sir John Mandeville*, supposedly the story of a British gentleman who had journeyed all over the world. According to one historian, "probably no book did more to arouse interest in travel and discovery, and to popularize the idea of a possible circumnavigation of the globe."[5] At the beginning, Mandeville's book was tak-

Ptolemy's map of the world from the second century contains those parts of the world he knew to exist and the latitude and longitude of each location. Although many relied on Ptolemy's calculations for more than a millennium, they were later proven to be highly inaccurate.

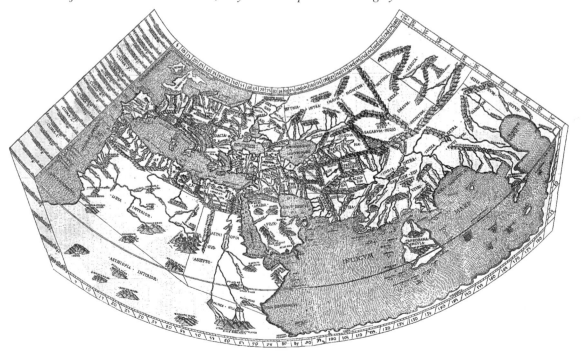

An illustration from the famous fourteenth-century work, The Travels of Sir John Mandeville. *The book's amazing tales, later found to be mostly fictional, inspired many adventurers to take to the seas in search of fabled lands of gold and riches.*

en to be true, but it retained its popularity long after the sixteenth-century voyages had proved much of it to be pure fiction. The author wrote:

> I, John Mandeville, Knight, . . . that was born in England, in the town of St. Albans, and passed [over] the sea in the year of our Lord Jesu Christ, 1322, in the day of St. Michael; and hitherto have been a long time over the sea, and have seen and gone through many diverse lands, and many provinces and kingdoms and isles and have passed throughout Turkey, Armenia the little and the great; through Tartary, Persia, Syria, Arabia, Egypt the high and the low; through Lybia, Chaldea, and a great part of Ethiopia; through Amazonia, Ind [India] the less and the more, a great part; and throughout many other Isles, that be about Ind.[6]

Mandeville perpetuated the story of Prester John and told how the king's tables were made of emeralds and other precious stones. He also told of China and described its wonders. The popularity of Mandeville's tale sparked the interest of many a young—and not-so-young—adventurer who hoped to see these glorious lands some day.

Experience: True Tales, or Almost True

During the eleventh and twelfth centuries, Europeans who fought in the Crusades traveled as far east as Constantinople and Jerusalem. Though exotic to those who stayed at home, these regions bordering on the Mediterranean were nevertheless part of the known world of the ancients. In the thirteenth century a new age of

The Land of Prester John

In the fourteenth century a fictional tale, The Travels of Sir John Mandeville, *was very popular among European readers, who thought it was a true account. In these excerpts, the author describes the wonderful land of the imaginary Christian king Prester John.*

"In the land of Prester John be many diverse things and many precious stones, so great and so large, that men make of them vessels, as platters, dishes and cups. . . . This emperor Prester John is Christian, and a great part of his country also. But yet, they have not all of the articles of our faith as we have. . . . And he hath under him seventy-two provinces, and in every province is a king. . . . And the principal gates of his palace be of precious stone that men clepe [call] sardonyx, and the border and the bars be of ivory. And the windows of the halls and chambers be of crystal. And the tables whereon men eat, some be of emeralds, some of amethyst, and some of gold, full of precious stones; and the pillars that bear up the tables be of the same precious stones."

travel began, after Genghis Khan conquered central Asia and established a well-administered reign over Eurasia from Poland eastward to the Pacific Ocean. The Mongols tolerated Christianity and welcomed traders from Europe. It was possible to travel safely and efficiently across most of Asia by this time. The capital city of the Mongols was known as Cambaluc, present-day Beijing.

The best-known Europeans to travel to China were the Polo brothers, Maffeo and Nicolo, of Venice, and Nicolo's teenage son, Marco. Among them, they spent most of the years from 1256 to 1292 in China and traveling between China and Venice. During that period, the great Kublai Khan was emperor of China, and he reportedly took a liking to young Marco, allowing him to travel as the khan's representative to the far reaches of the kingdom.

Kublai Khan died in 1294, and in the power struggle that followed, Europeans were discouraged from traveling to China. Meanwhile, Marco Polo had returned to Italy but was captured and jailed in Genoa, a casualty of the fierce rivalry between that city-state and Polo's native Venice. While in prison, Marco Polo wrote a book telling of his adventures in China. His book was widely read, but many people thought it was just another wild tale. Europeans found it hard to believe that an advanced civilization could exist outside of their own. In fact, Polo's book is not completely accurate. He relied on tales from other travelers in the court of the khan, and his interpretation of certain events and places is suspect. Nevertheless, much of what he had written was true, and, in any case, his book fueled the desire of Europeans to reach China by an easier means than the year-long journey across the continent. Additionally, Polo's somewhat-informed estimates of the size of China, as well as the distance between China and Japan, helped to persuade Columbus that the land was close enough to reach by a short trip to the west.

The Positive Climate

Europe in the late fifteenth century was a society poised to take giant steps into the future. There were a number of factors that made possible the great adventures of exploration and discovery that were to come. Prosperity; missionary zeal; advances in shipbuilding, navigation, and mapmaking; and the very nature of the explorers and their crews all made the voyages possible and even inevitable.

During the fourteenth century, a third of Europe's population had died from bubonic plague, in an epidemic known as the black death. It was a great loss of life, but, as a result, the survivors had more room to spread out and more food to eat and were, consequently, healthier.

In the meantime, what had previously been land routes to the East were barred to Europeans. China was off-limits after the defeat of Kublai Khan's descendants in 1368, and the rise of the Ottoman Empire in Turkey put up yet another boundary between East and West. Yet because of the experience of the past and because of the popular stories, everyone knew that great riches existed in the East, and the profit motive was strong.

In addition, a desire to make converts to Christianity motivated many. The Crusades had not been a particularly successful venture, and most of the Middle East remained under Islamic control. China, it was known, was not Christian at all. Thus much of the world beckoned as prime territory for Christian missionaries.

Two members of the Polo family visit Kublai Khan in China. Marco Polo's writings about his adventures later inspired many Europeans, including Columbus, to try to find a quicker route to China.

Until the fifteenth century, sailing had been primarily a coastal affair. Indeed, the sailors on the Mediterranean rarely ventured out of sight of land. They knew the waters quite well, however. Over the years, they had accumulated detailed data on coastal features, winds, and currents, which they passed along to others. Not just in Europe, but all over the world, sailors were making remarkable voyages. In the Pacific Ocean, in the waters around India and Africa, and in the North Atlantic, brave sailors—whose names will never be known—discovered new lands and often settled them. In most cases, however, their watercraft depended upon winds and currents to carry them forward; returning home could be a difficult or even impossible task. The European explorers of the fifteenth and sixteenth centuries, however, were interested not merely in finding new lands, but in profiting from them. As historian John R. Hale says, "There was no point in finding a new market or source of wealth if news of it could not be brought home."[7]

Shipbuilding in the fifteenth century drew on the experience of two separate traditions, "one producing the stout, broad, square-sailed trader of the North Sea and the Atlantic Coast, the other the oared galleys and lateen [triangular]-rigged coasters

The Wonders of Japan

The Travels of Marco Polo *was a popular and influential book during the fourteenth and fifteenth centuries. Although Polo never went to Japan, he describes it here, basing his account on stories he heard from others. His incorrect placement of Japan in relation to China greatly influenced Columbus. This selection is from a modern translation by Teresa Waugh.*

"Japan is an island in the middle of the Ocean, 1,500 miles from the mainland. It is a vast island whose inhabitants have white skins and beautiful manners. . . . Gold is mined there in huge quantities. Nobody ever goes to Japan from the mainland so the gold never leaves the island. . . . The ruler of Japan has a magnificent palace roofed entirely with fine gold. . . . It would be almost impossible to estimate the value of this gold. But besides the roof, the floors of the bedrooms are covered with a layer of gold, two fingers thick.

The island of Japan lies in the China Sea, in other words the sea beside Manzi, for China is called Manzi in their language. It is an eastern sea. In it lie, according to the most experienced sailors, some 7,448 islands, most of which are inhabited. On each of these islands there are very sweetly-scented trees whose timber is as useful, if not more so, than aloe wood. There is also a vast quantity of pepper as white as snow, as well as a considerable amount of black pepper."

of the Mediterranean."[8] The ships were also equipped with heavy artillery, which made conquest efficient. Since the explorers intended from the start to create markets and profit from their new discoveries, they needed to be prepared to deal with opposition.

Sailors were by nature a risk-taking lot. They certainly knew that their chances of returning from a long voyage were only about fifty-fifty. Diseases of malnutrition—such as scurvy (from lack of vitamin C) and beriberi (from lack of vitamin B)—killed many, and injuries were frequently fatal in the unsanitary confines of a ship. Still, ordinary seamen continued to enlist. Perhaps they concluded that their chances were not much worse at sea than on land. The average fifteenth-century man lived only about thirty years, and diseases were prevalent everywhere, on land as well as at sea. Life was hard for farmers and craftsmen as well as for sailors, so the choice to go to sea was likely just a matter of individual disposition. Whatever the reasons, the captains of the voyages of exploration rarely had any trouble finding enough seamen to fill their rosters.

Henry the Navigator

The man who came to be known as Henry the Navigator was not in fact much of a seaman at all. He was Prince Henry of Portugal, a younger son of King João (John) I. João had married an English princess, Philippa of Lancaster, daughter of John of Gaunt. Henry was born in 1394 and grew to resemble the English side of the family, tall and blond. He was, according to a modern historian, "brave in heart, keen in

Although not a seaman, Henry the Navigator earned his title because of the many voyages of exploration that he so ably planned and organized from his headquarters in Sagres, and for his adventurous and brave spirit.

mind, and noble in spirit."[9] In 1415, when he was only twenty-one years old, Henry went with his father on a battle to capture the Muslim city of Ceuta in Morocco. After the Portuguese victory, Henry stayed on awhile in Morocco and learned of the trade in valuable goods that had gone on for years in Africa. In particular, he learned about the continent's western "Gold Coast," where many valuable metals could be found. It is likely that Prince Henry calculated that even if a good long-term goal was to find a passage to India, a good short-term goal would be to establish a lucrative Africa trade.

Henry watches the return of an expedition from the window of his observatory, which he staffed with numerous scientists and mathematicians, including astronomers, mapmakers, and physicians.

In 1418 Prince Henry's father made him governor of Algarve, the southernmost territory of Portugal. There, on the western edge of Europe, near the village of Sagres, Henry set up a palace where he would live for the rest of his life. He built an observatory there and proceeded to hire astronomers, physicians, mapmakers, and other scientists and mathematicians. Sagres became the headquarters for the great ventures of exploration that Prince Henry had in mind.

Henry's first step was to colonize the islands of the Atlantic, most of which had been explored during the previous cen-

tury. The ancients had known of the Canaries, while it was probably sailors from Genoa who had discovered Madeira and the Azores. Henry sent colonists to Madeira in 1420, and in attempting to clear the thick forests on the island, they started a forest fire, which reportedly raged for seven years. Afterward, however, grapes were brought in from Crete and thrived in the ash-rich ground. Madeira has been known ever since for its fine wine.

Several voyages to Grand Canary in the 1420s were intended to colonize that island as well but resulted chiefly in information about the island group and its surrounding waters. This information would be invaluable to the next generation of Portuguese sailors. The exploration of the Azores followed in the 1430s, and by the 1440s Portuguese colonists were well established there.

The African Coast

Meanwhile, Henry was learning more and more about the African coast. Each year he sent a few vessels out to go as far south along the coast as they could and return with information. At that time, the great barrier to further exploration was Cape Bojador. As we look at modern maps, it seems difficult to believe that this feature, now generally called Cap Boujdour, was such an obstacle to sailors. It is a very slight bulge on the west coast, just barely south of the Canary Islands. Some of the difficulties were physical, such as treacherous currents and reefs that extended well out to sea. However, for the most part it was, in the words of historian Daniel Boorstin, "a barrier in the mind."[10] The sailors believed that beyond this point lay the Sea of Darkness, "and beyond too, lay the torrid zone, in which white men would become black."[11]

Prince Henry sent out at least fifteen expeditions to round Cape Bojador. Each one returned without succeeding. The reasons for failure were varied and imaginative, but in the end they amounted to excuses. In 1433 Henry sent Gil Eannes, one of his most experienced captains, and a man whom he knew well. On this first try, Eannes also returned empty-handed, but Henry was determined and sent him back the following year. On this occasion, in 1434, Eannes sailed farther out to sea than usual, and when he turned to the south, he discovered that he had already passed the cape. He landed on the coast and took a look around. In the words of contemporary chronicler Gomes Eanes de Zurara:

> In that voyage he doubled the Cape, despising all danger, and found the lands beyond quite contrary to what he, like others, had expected. And although the matter was a small one in itself, yet on account of its daring it was reckoned great.[12]

Not One Who Dared

Gomes Eanes de Zurara, a fifteenth-century writer, explains why the mariners of his time were reluctant to sail past Cape Bojador on the coast of North Africa. This excerpt is from his book The Chronicle of the Discovery and Conquest of Guinea.

"This much you may learn, that although he [Prince Henry the Navigator] sent out many times, not only ordinary men, but such as . . . were of foremost name in the profession of arms, yet there was not one who dared to pass that Cape of Bojador and learn about the land beyond it. . . . And to say the truth this was not from cowardice or want of good will, but from the novelty of the thing and the wide-spread and ancient rumour about this Cape, that had been cherished by the mariners of Spain from generation to generation . . . being satisfied of the peril, and seeing no hope of honor or profit, they left off the attempt. For, said the mariners, this much is clear, that beyond this Cape there is no race of men nor place of inhabitants; nor is the land less sandy than the deserts of Libya, where there is no water, no tree, no green herb—and the sea so shallow . . . while the currents are so terrible that no ship having once passed the Cape, will ever be able to return. . . . Now what sort of a ship's captain would he be who, with such doubts placed before him . . . and with such certain prospect of death before his eyes, could venture the trial of such a bold feat as that?"

That was all it took. The next year Eannes went out again, this time going even farther down the coast. Bit by bit, over the next few years, Portuguese sailors explored farther and farther along the coast of Africa, passing Cabo Blanco (Cap Blanc) and exploring the Bay of Arguin. In the 1440s the Portuguese were distracted from the goals of exploration by a profitable new enterprise begun along the coast of Africa: the slave trade. Two of Prince Henry's captains, Nuno Tristão and Antão Gonçalves, brought the first load of Africans to Portugal to be sold as slaves in 1441. According to Zurara's eyewitness account, "Mothers would clasp their infants in their arms, and throw themselves on the ground to cover them with their bodies, disregarding any injury to their own persons, so that they could prevent their children from being separated from them."[13] Zurara maintained, however, that the slaves were treated well and that within a few years most of the original group had learned trades, married Portuguese citizens, and were in effect absorbed into the general Portuguese society. Still, it was the beginning of European participation in a profitable but cruel trade in human lives that would continue for over four hundred years.

In 1445 Dinas Dias reached the Senegal River and gave the name Cape Verde to what he correctly surmised was the westernmost point of Africa. During the next few years, the Portuguese were content to exploit the lands they had already explored. Trading and slaving kept twenty-five Portuguese ships busy every year. In the mid-1450s, Alvise da Cadamosto, a Venetian who sailed for Prince Henry, got as far as the Gambia River and even spent several months inland. His reports included the first observation of the stars using the Southern Cross as a guide point. He spent some time with several native tribes and reported about the exotic plant and animal life that he found there.

The Legacy of Henry the Navigator

Prince Henry died in 1460, at the age of sixty-six. His plans went ahead, however. Just after he died, one of his men, Pedro de Sintra, took two small sailing ships called caravels and sailed 350 miles farther down the coast than any Portuguese before him. He explored the coast of present-day Sierra Leone and Liberia. Certainly finding the way around Africa was only a matter of time.

In 1473 another great obstacle was crossed, and the Portuguese were a step closer to rounding Africa: Lopo Gonçalves and a crew sailed south of the equator. Somewhat to their amazement, they did not burst into flames or turn black from the intense heat. In 1481 King João II sent Diogo Cão on a series of voyages with the express intention of finding a sea route to India around Africa. Cão took with him several large stone pillars, called *padrões*, which he was to set up at strategic locations, to claim the lands for Portugal. Over several years and several voyages, Cão sailed south as far as Cape Cross, in present-day Namibia. He set up one of his *padrões* at the mouth of the great Congo River but fell far short of rounding the continent.

In late 1487 King João sent out yet another expedition with the intent of circumnavigating, or sailing completely around, Africa. There were three ships under the command of Bartolomeu Dias. Chance aided Dias: When he was about 520 miles northwest of the tip of Africa, a violent storm blew the ships out to sea. They were tossed about for days, and when they finally found their way back to land, in early January 1488, they were at Mossel Bay, on the eastward side of the cape. Dias continued to sail northeastward up the coast of Africa until his men began to panic and forced him to turn around. As they passed the tip of Africa for the second time—on this occasion actually seeing it—Dias named

Why Explore?

Gomes Eanes de Zurara tells why Prince Henry the Navigator sent out ships of exploration along the African coast. This excerpt is from his Chronicle of the Discovery and Conquest of Guinea.

"He was stirred up by his zeal for the service of God and of the King Edward his Lord and brother, who then reigned. And this was the first reason for his action.

The second reason was that . . . many kinds of merchandise might be brought to this realm, which would find a ready market, and reasonably so, because no other people of these parts traded with them; . . . and also the products of this realm might be taken there, which traffic would bring great profit to our countrymen.

The third reason was that, as it was said that the power of the Moors [Muslims] in that land of Africa was very much greater than was commonly supposed, and that there were no Christians among them. . . . [Prince Henry] exerted himself to make it known . . . how far the power of those infidels [non-Christians] extended.

The fourth reason was . . . [that] he sought to know if there were in those parts any Christian princes, in whom the charity and the love of Christ was so ingrained that they would aid him against those enemies of the faith.

The fifth reason was his great desire to make increase in the faith of our Lord Jesus Christ and to bring to him all the souls that should be saved."

Henry sent expeditions to the African coast for many reasons, including Christianity and the lure of a lucrative trade.

INDEPENDENCE HIGH SCHOOL LIBRARY

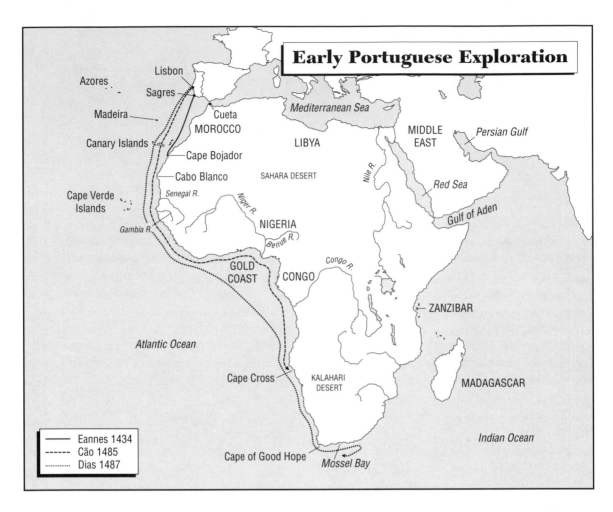

Early Portuguese Exploration

Azores
Lisbon
Sagres
Madeira
Canary Islands
Cueta
MOROCCO
LIBYA
Mediterranean Sea
MIDDLE
EAST
Persian Gulf
Cape Bojador
Cabo Blanco
SAHARA DESERT
Nile R.
Red Sea
Cape Verde
Islands
Senegal R.
Gulf of Aden
Gambia R.
Niger R.
NIGERIA
Benue R.
GOLD
COAST
CONGO
Congo R.
ZANZIBAR
Atlantic Ocean
Cape Cross
KALAHARI
DESERT
MADAGASCAR
Indian Ocean
Cape of Good Hope
Mossel Bay

— Eannes 1434
- - - Cão 1485
.... Dias 1487

it the Cape of Storms. But King João, as historian J. R. Hale says, "looked to the future which Dias had made possible and renamed it the Cape of Good Hope."[14]

Prince Henry the Navigator left Portugal a legacy of seafaring and discovery that kept the country in the forefront of European powers for several hundred years. It was Henry's organization and planning that started the age of European discovery and exploration. In the words of historian J. H. Parry:

Prince Henry and his brother Prince Pedro, by placing gentlemen of their households in command of some of the ships and demanding from them longer voyages, more detailed reports, more captives to be converted or enslaved, and higher returns, gave energy and direction to a movement of maritime expansion which probably would have taken place in any event, but which might for many years have been confined to fishing and casual slaving.[15]

Chapter

2 The Enterprise of the Indies: Christopher Columbus

Five hundred years after Christopher Columbus's voyages, it is fashionable to discount his accomplishments, saying that he was not the first European to "discover" the Americas, and to depict him as cruel, unfeeling, and slightly stupid. In fact, he was a very complicated man, and he is important to history because his voyages were not a dead end, but rather led directly to the first permanent European colony in America and to dramatic changes in the way of life of Europeans and native American peoples alike. Europeans would have "discovered" the Americas before long in any case. That it was Columbus who did it first is a credit to his single-mindedness, his dedication to an ideal, his leadership abilities, and his seamanship.

A Genoese Sailor

In September or October 1451, Christoforo Colombo was born in Genoa, the son and grandson of woolen weavers. There are no portraits of him that date from his lifetime, and most of those that do exist contradict one another. However, his own younger son, Fernando, provides what may be the most reliable description available to modern readers:

A well-built man of average height; his face was long, with rather high cheekbones, and his body neither fat nor lean. His nose was aquiline [narrow and somewhat hooked], his eyes light in color, and his complexion fresh and ruddy [reddish]. His hair was fair when he was young, but turned grey when he was thirty.[16]

As a boy, he had little or no schooling, but rather spent his time helping his father in the family woolen trade. He may have spent some time on local ships in the Mediterranean but likely did not become a sailor until sometime in the 1470s, when he was a grown man.

In 1476, when he was twenty-five years old, Columbus sailed with a convoy of goods to Lisbon, England, and Flanders. Off Portugal, a French fleet attacked the convoy and sank the ship Columbus was on. Buoyed by a piece of the broken ship, he swam to shore, landing at Lagos. Apparently, he liked Portugal, because he made his way to Lisbon, where, according to Fernando, there were "many of his Genoese countrymen," and there he stayed.[17] Three years later, he was a master mariner and had married a Portuguese woman, the daughter of a well-known seaman. Within a year of his marriage, he had a son, Diego, and the young family moved to the

An able leader and sailor, Christopher Columbus became determined to discover lands west of the Canary Islands that he was sure existed.

island of Madeira, in the Atlantic off the coast of Portugal. By this time, his father-in-law had died and his mother-in-law gave Columbus all of her late husband's sea charts.

Although Prince Henry the Navigator was dead, his brother, King João II, continued to pursue the route to the Indies around Africa. Spain had recognized Portugal's rights to the African coast, and the Portuguese were doing a good trade in gold and slaves. It appears that Columbus went on at least one of these Portuguese trading and exploration missions between 1482 and 1484. It was at this time that he began to devote all of his time and attention to what he referred to as the Enterprise of the Indies—a phrase that bears

some explaining. In the early days of the age of exploration, "the Indies" meant modern China, Japan, Thailand, and Indonesia, as well as all the other island groups in the region bounded on the west by the subcontinent of India. Later, the terms "West Indies" and "East Indies" would be applied to the islands of the Caribbean and the islands of the northern Pacific, respectively.

Columbus's idea was to find a short sea route to the Indies, possibly discovering an island to be used as a staging area on the way. The future explorer had learned to read and write during his stay in Portugal, and he did a tremendous amount of research in pursuit of his goal. His sources ranged from Aristotle to *Imago Mundi* and the Bible. His copies of many of these works, with underlines and handwritten marginal notes, are available today to scholars.

Columbus was by this time in the prime of his life. He was an experienced sailor and an experienced leader. He knew well that it was possible to sail beyond the bounds of the Mediterranean. He began to speculate about other possibilities. According to Fernando:

> While he was in Portugal [Columbus] began to speculate that if the Portuguese could sail so far southward, it should be possible to sail just as far to the west, and that one might expect to find land in that direction. . . . He grew convinced beyond doubt that west of the Canaries and the Cape Verdes many lands lay waiting to be discovered.[18]

Still, in order to reach these other lands, a great deal of planning and calculation was first necessary.

The Size of the Earth

Columbus never would have sailed west in hopes of reaching Japan and China had he not both underestimated the circumference of the globe and overestimated the landmass of Asia. Although he used Ptolemy's estimate that the earth was 18,000 miles in circumference and that each degree of longitude was about 50 miles at the equator, Columbus concluded from his reading that the ancient astronomer had underestimated the length of the Asian continent. Thus, he then added more distance to represent the lands described by Marco Polo, and even more for the distance that Polo had estimated between mainland China and Japan. Further, Columbus planned to start from the westernmost point of the Canary Islands. That left a crossing of only 60° between the Canaries and Japan, but even that was extremely long—certainly farther than anyone had ever sailed nonstop.

But the goal was becoming tantalizingly close, and Columbus continued to calculate. If a degree of longitude was 50 nautical miles at the equator, he reasoned, then it would be only about 40 nautical miles at 28° north latitude (28° N), the point from which he proposed to cross. Thus the total distance from the Canaries to Japan would only be 2,400 nautical miles, a manageable distance. The actual airline distance from the Canaries to Japan is 10,600 miles, so Columbus's estimate was wildly erroneous. As it happened, however, the figure of 2,400 miles is a surprisingly accurate estimate of the distance between the Canaries and the islands that we now know as the West Indies.

The Long Wait

Having convinced himself of the practicality of the voyage, Columbus now had to convince others. In particular, he had to find a sponsor—someone who would pay for the ships, equipment, and sailors needed to make the voyage a reality. Logically enough, he applied first, in 1484, to King

Columbus demonstrates his theory that the distance from the Canaries to Japan is 2,400 miles, an erroneous calculation that is less than one-fourth of the actual distance.

João II of Portugal, hoping that the Portuguese tradition of exploration would help his cause. The king referred Columbus to an advisory commission, which "dismissed him politely but firmly, considering his plan 'as vain, simply founded on imagination.'"[19] In any case, Portugal was fully engaged in the Africa trade.

At this point, there was nothing left for Columbus in Portugal. His wife had died, and the Portuguese were not interested in his enterprise. Columbus had two brothers, however: Diego and Bartholomew; the latter was a mapmaker who supported Christopher's idea. When the Portuguese were not interested, Bartholomew set off for England and France to attempt to gain support from one of those nations. Meanwhile, in 1485 Columbus took his young son Diego and went to Spain. He left Diego to be educated at a Franciscan monastery in Palos and took himself to the royal city of Cordova to put his plan before Ferdinand and Isabella, the Spanish monarchs of Aragon and Castile.

It was a long and tedious prospect. Columbus waited almost a year before he had his first audience with the queen. Isabella was interested in the idea and appointed a special commission to examine it and give her a recommendation. Then Columbus had to wait some more. For the next six years, he waited, with only occasional royal audiences to keep his hopes alive. According to biographer Morison, this was

> the most unhappy period in Columbus's life. . . . A proud, sensitive man who *knew* that his project would open fresh paths to wealth and for the advancement of Christ's kingdom, he had to endure clownish witticisms and

crackpot jests by ignorant courtiers, to be treated like a beggar; even at times to suffer want.[20]

When nothing had happened by 1488, Columbus decided to try King João again. He and Bartholomew arranged to have an audience with the king, but before it could take place, Bartolomeu Dias sailed triumphantly into Lisbon, having rounded the Cape of Good Hope and sailed well up the east coast of Africa. The Portuguese were now assured of an eastern route to Asia; Columbus's western voyage was no longer of any interest at all.

Queen Isabella's commission finally came back with a recommendation in 1490, but it was not favorable to Columbus. They concluded that the project "rested on weak foundations" and that it seemed "uncertain and impossible to any educated person."[21] Further, they argued, according to Morison, "that the Ocean was infinitely larger than Columbus supposed, and much of it [was] unnavigable. And finally, God would never have allowed any uninhabited land of real value to be concealed from His people for so many centuries!"[22]

Take It or Leave It

Columbus was deeply disappointed but no less certain of his enterprise. Queen Isabella must have seen both his certainty and his disappointment, for she told him that he could apply again when Spain's war with the Moors was over. He waited a year. The war was still going on, but Columbus was impatient. His demands were growing larger all the time, too, as both his certainty and his anger grew. In

Columbus attempts to persuade Ferdinand and Isabella of Spain to finance his western voyage to the Indies. While at first Columbus's requests were denied, a royal aide later successfully urged the queen to reconsider her decision.

late December 1491 he appeared before both Ferdinand and Isabella, and now he wanted not only ships and supplies, but also titles and honors, as well as a cut of any trade that resulted from his voyage. Morison describes the scene:

> He had suffered so many insults and outrages during his long residence in Spain that—by San Fernando!—he would not glorify Spain for nothing. If the Sovereigns [king and queen] would grant him, contingent on his success, such rank, titles, and property that he and his issue [children and grandchildren] could hold up their heads with the Spanish nobility, well and good; but no more bargaining. Take it, Your Majesties, or leave it.[23]

They refused him, and Columbus packed his things and prepared to leave Spain and start all over again with the king of France. He was actually on his way when Luis de Santángel, one of the queen's advisers, urged the queen to give Columbus his chance, and she did, offering to pledge her crown jewels to pay for the enterprise if it should be necessary.

The First Voyage

The spring of 1492 was a busy and happy time for Columbus. He went to Palos in southern Spain to prepare for the voyage. There he hired three vessels, along with crews for them. Two of the ships, the *Niña*

Columbus's three ships, the Pinta, *the* Niña, *and the* Santa María, *carrying a total crew of ninety men, set sail out of Palos, Spain, on August 3, 1492.*

and the *Pinta*, were caravels. The flagship *Santa María* was a larger, square-rigged ship. Columbus himself was captain of the *Santa María*, and the owner, Juan de la Cosa, came along as master, with Peralonso Niño as pilot. The captain of the *Pinta* was Martín Alonso Pinzón, and its master was Francisco Pinzón. Vincente Yáñez Pinzón was the captain of the *Niña*, and its owner and pilot was Juan Niño. All these men were sailors of some experience and skill, and as their names suggest, most of them were related. The captain's role on the ship was as an overall leader. The master was responsible for the business aspects of the ship: loading and unloading cargo, buying supplies, keeping accounts. The pilot was something like a combination navigator and first mate. Altogether, there were about ninety men on the three ships, eighty-seven of whom can be identified by name.

They left Spain on August 3, 1492, but did not immediately strike out into the unknown sea. The original intention was to sail to Grand Canary and sail west on that latitude, but the *Pinta* needed repairs—Columbus suspected sabotage—and it was not until September 6 that the ships actually set out. The weather was fine, and they had good winds blowing them westward. On September 9, Columbus recorded in his journal, "We sailed sixteen and a half leagues. I have decided to log less than our true run, so that if the voyage is long the crew will not be afraid and lose heart."[24]

Within a few weeks, they began seeing what Columbus interpreted as signs that they were near land: weeds and birds. The men, however, were not convinced. By October 10, they had already been at sea longer than anyone ever had before. Columbus reassured them: He was certain they would find land within days. On the night of October 11, Columbus records that he saw "what I thought was a light. . . . Only a few people thought it was a sign of land, but I was sure we were close to a landfall."[25] At two o'clock on the morning of October 12, Rodrigo de Triana on lookout on the *Pinta* sighted land. At daybreak, Columbus and some of the others went ashore. Columbus relates the story:

> We saw naked people, and I went ashore in a boat with armed men, taking Martín Alonso Pinzón and his brother Vicente Yáñez, captain of the *Niña*. I took the royal standard, and the captains each took a banner with the Green Cross which each of my ships carries as a device, with the letters F and Y [for Ferdinand and Isabella (Ysabela)], surmounted by a crown, at each end of the cross. . . . Soon many of the islanders gathered round us. . . . Wishing them to look upon us with friendship I gave some of them red bonnets and glass beads which they hung round their necks, and many other things of small value, at which they were so delighted and so eager to please us that we could not believe it.[26]

It was the island in the Bahamas known as San Salvador, or Watling Island. Columbus, convinced he was near "the Indies," called the inhabitants "Indians." He knew that this small island was not what he was looking for, however, and spent several

The Beginning of Columbus's Voyage

In this selection from The Voyage of Christopher Columbus: Columbus's Own Journal of Discovery, *translated by John Cummins, Columbus tells of the decision to send him on his first voyage and of the beginning of that voyage.*

"Your Majesties [Ferdinand and Isabella], being Catholic Christians and rulers devoted to the Holy Christian Faith . . . decided to send me, Christopher Columbus, to those lands of India to meet their rulers and to see the towns and lands . . . and to find out in what manner they might be converted to our Holy Faith; and you ordered me not to go eastward by land, as is customary, but to take my course westward, where, so far as we know, no man has travelled before today. . . .

I left the city of Granada on Saturday, 12 May 1492, and travelled to the port of Palos, where I prepared three vessels well suited for such an enterprise. I left that port, amply furnished with provisions and well crewed with seafaring men, on Friday, 3 August, sailing for Your Majesties' Canary Islands in the Ocean Sea, intending to set my course from there and sail until I reach the Indies, where I will convey Your Majesties' embassy to those rulers and so carry out my orders."

days sailing around the nearby islands, landing and meeting the natives, who called themselves the Taino people. Some of the Taino, he noticed, wore small gold ornaments, and this confirmed to Columbus that he was near China and Japan.

By means of sign language, the locals informed Columbus that there was a much larger island to the south; they called it Colba, or Cuba. Columbus, convinced that he was on the easternmost edges of Asia, deduced that the large island was Cipango, or Japan. In his journal, he wrote, "I shall set off for another, very large island which I think must be Cipangu, judging by the indications given me by these Indians I

A Cagey Ruse

In this excerpt from Columbus's journal of the first voyage, translated by John Cummins, Columbus describes how he decided to keep from the men the facts about how far away from Europe they had actually sailed. We are not told whether his men, who were experienced sailors, were deceived by this tactic.

"Sunday, 9 September. We sailed sixteen and a half leagues. I have decided to log less than our true run, so that if the voyage is long the crew will not be afraid and lose heart.

Wednesday, 26 September. Sailed on course W until after noon, then SW until we found that what we had thought was land was only clouds. Our twenty-four hour run was about thirty-three leagues; I told the men twenty-five and a half. The sea was just like a river, with sweet, gentle breezes.

Thursday, 27 September. On course W, about twenty-five and a half leagues in the twenty-four hours. I told the men twenty-one. We saw many *dorados* [giltheads, or other gold-colored fish], and one was killed. We also saw a tropic bird.

Wednesday, 10 October. Sailed WSW at about eight knots, sometimes up to nine and a half, occasionally only five and a half. Sixty-two and a half leagues in the twenty-four hours; I told the men only forty-six and a half. They could contain themselves no longer, and began to complain of the length of the voyage. I encouraged them as best I could, trying to raise their hopes of benefits they might gain from it. I also told them that it was useless to complain; having set out for the Indies I shall continue this voyage until, with God's grace, I reach them."

After sailing for more than a month, Columbus and his crew come ashore on the island of San Salvador in the Bahamas. Instead of reaching Japan and China, as he had hoped, Columbus's journeys took him to the Bahamas, Cuba, and Hispaniola.

have on board. They call it Colba, and say that there are many big ships there, and seafarers, and that it is very large."[27]

Columbus sighted Cuba on October 27 and spent several weeks sailing along its northern coast. It was, he noted, "the most beautiful island ever seen, full of fine harbors and deep rivers." He was looking for large cities and for the palace of the Great Khan, but he found only small villages, composed of huts. He never found a city or a king, but his men did come across something that would have an enormous impact on Europe and on the world: tobacco. On November 6, Columbus notes, "My two men met many people crossing their path to reach their villages, men and women, carrying in their hand a burning brand and herbs which they use to produce fragrant smoke."[28]

Columbus spent two more months sailing around the Bahamas, Cuba, and Hispaniola (present-day Haiti and the Dominican Republic). Early Christmas morning, the *Santa María* ran aground just off Cap Haitien (in present-day Haiti). Columbus was unable to save the ship, but all of the men and most of the stores were saved. The wood from the *Santa María* was used to build a fort, and Columbus left forty men there to maintain it, the first European settlement in the Americas in modern times.

At this point, Columbus determined that it was time to get back to Spain, to report his discoveries. His journey would be useless if no one at home ever knew about it. The two caravels had a good, fast voyage for the first few weeks, sailing east and north and crossing most of the Atlantic at a latitude of prevailing westerly winds.

They ran into terrible storms as they neared Europe, however, and arrived somewhat worse for the wear in Lisbon Harbor on March 3, 1493.

Triumphant Return

In April Ferdinand and Isabella received Columbus at their court in Barcelona. He had already sent them a letter detailing his triumphs and his expectations that much gold and many spices were to be found. When Columbus arrived at court, in company with several Taino he had brought back from the Indies, the monarchs were delighted to grant him the titles and privileges he had requested before the voyage, and he was afterward known as Admiral of the Ocean Sea and Viceroy of the Indies.

Ferdinand and Isabella agreed without hesitation to send Columbus back so that he could make even greater discoveries, including, they hoped, the court of the Great Khan and, more importantly, sources of gold. To be certain that any gold discovered would belong to Spain, the monarchs applied to Pope Alexander VI for the rights to trade and conquest in these newly discovered lands. The pope, acting in a customary role as the final authority on matters of worldwide (that is, European) importance, had to decide between Spain's claim and that of Portugal, which had earlier received rights "in the Ocean Sea [Atlantic] towards the regions lying southward and eastward." They interpreted this as "full title to the whole of the Atlantic south of the Canary Islands."[29] Pope Alexander was not exactly an impartial judge; he was partly Spanish, and Ferdinand and Isabella had supported him in his bid for the papacy.

Upon his return, Columbus is greeted with a royal reception from Ferdinand and Isabella, who agreed to finance future voyages in search of gold, spices, and even greater discoveries.

The pope followed the suggestion of Ferdinand and Isabella, and in 1493 he set a vertical line of demarcation 100 leagues (about 300 miles) west of the Azores, granting Spain the lands west of this line that were not already subject to another Christian ruler. Portugal naturally objected, and in 1494 Spain and Portugal compromised with the Treaty of Tordesillas, which moved the line of demarcation another 270 leagues west. The primary result of this treaty was to give Portugal an eventual claim to Brazil, which lies east of the line.

Columbus made three more trips to the West Indies over the next ten years. On his second voyage, he came upon the Windward and Leeward Islands, naming them as he went: Santa Maria de Guadalupe, Santa Maria de Monserrate (Montserrat), San Martín (Nevis), San Jorge (Saint Kitts), Santa Cruz (Saint Croix), San

Columbus's Triumphant Return

Bartolomé de Las Casas describes the reception Columbus received from Ferdinand and Isabella when he returned to Spain in April 1493, in this selection from Witness: The Writings of Bartolomé de Las Casas, *edited and translated by George Sanderlin.*

"Don Christopher Columbus hurried as fast as possible to reach Barcelona, where he arrived in the middle of April—and the sovereigns were very anxious to see him. When it was known that he was arriving, they ordered that he be given a solemn and very beautiful welcome, for which the entire city came out, so that there was not room for all the people in the streets. All wondered to see that venerable person who was said to have discovered another world; to see the Indians, parrots, jewels, and gold things he had discovered and was bringing, things never before seen or heard of. . . .

Then Don Christopher Columbus entered the square, where the sovereigns were accompanied by a multitude of gentlemen and nobles. Amongst them all, as he had a lofty and authoritative bearing, like that of a Roman senator, his venerable countenance [face], gray hair, and modest smile stood out, expressing well the joy and glory with which he came."

Columbus receives a hero's welcome from the entire city of Barcelona. For his accomplishments, Ferdinand and Isabella honored Columbus with the titles Admiral of the Ocean Sea and Viceroy of the Indies.

Juan Bautista (Puerto Rico), and others. At Hispaniola he found that the islanders had killed every member of the crew he had left behind at the fort made from the *Santa María*'s timbers.

On the third voyage, in 1498, Columbus landed on Trinidad and then, a few days later, on a beach formed by the delta of the Orinoco River, in present-day Venezuela. Although at first he thought this was yet another island, the size and power of the river changed his mind. He wrote, "I believe that this is a very great continent, which until today has been unknown."[30] But because he was still convinced he was somewhere near China, he concluded that this landmass must be the Earthly Paradise, the Garden of Eden. The medieval writers quoted in *Imago Mundi* said that the Garden of Eden was "at the furthest point of the Far East, where the sun rose on the day of creation."[31] Nevertheless, Columbus did recognize it as an "*otro mundo*," other world, and reported to Ferdinand and Isabella:

> And your Highnesses will gain these vast lands, which are an Other World, and where Christianity will have so much enjoyment, and our faith in time so great an increase. I say this with very honest intent and because I desire that your Highnesses may be the greatest lords in the world, lords of it all, I say; and that all may be with much service to and satisfaction of the Holy Trinity.[32]

The trip was not an unqualified success, however. On the second voyage, Columbus

The Treaty of Tordesillas

The Portuguese were dissatisfied with the line of demarcation determined by Pope Alexander VI's letter "Inter Caetera" in 1493. He appealed to Spain, and they agreed on the terms of the Treaty of Tordesillas, which ultimately gave Portugal a claim to Brazil. This excerpt is from Documents of American History, *edited by Henry Steele Commager.*

"Whereas a certain controversy exists between the King of Portugal [and] the King and Queen of Castile, Aragon, etc. . . . they agreed that a boundary or straight line be determined and drawn north and south, from pole to pole, on the . . . ocean sea from the Arctic to the Antarctic pole. [The] boundary or line shall be drawn straight . . . at a distan[ce] of three hundred seventy leagues west of the Cape Verde Islands. . . . All lands, both islands and mainlands, found and discovered already, or to be found or discovered hereafter, by the said King of Portugal and by his vessels on this side of the said line . . . shall belong to . . . the King of Portugal and his successors. All other lands, both islands and mainlands . . . found or to be found hereafter, . . . by the said King and Queen of Castile, Aragon, etc., and by their vessels, on the western side . . . shall belong to the said King and Queen . . . and to their successors."

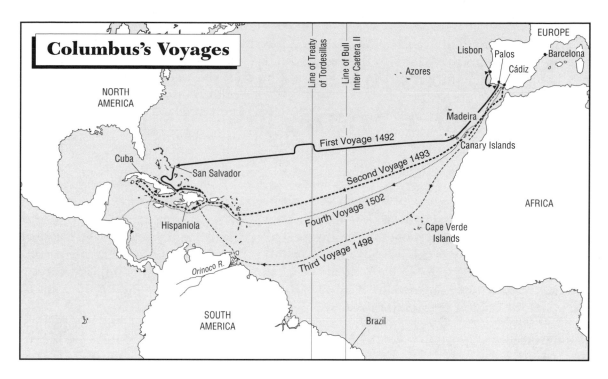

Columbus's Voyages

had left his brother Diego in charge of a group of colonists at Isabela, on Hispaniola. On the third voyage, he replaced Diego with his other brother, Bartholomew. The colonists were unruly, however, fighting one another when they were not fighting the natives. By this time, ships were regularly traveling between Spain and Hispaniola, and when word of the troubled colony reached Queen Isabella, she sent out a colonial governor named Bobadilla. Bobadilla promptly took charge, and in October 1500 he arrested all three Columbus brothers and sent them back to Spain in chains.

The queen, however, was not prepared to be too hard on the admiral. She freed Columbus and sent him on a fourth and final voyage in 1502. On that voyage, Columbus sailed near the Central American coast, still looking for a passage to India. The trip was a difficult one, and even on the way home, the crew became stranded for a year on Jamaica because their ships leaked so badly. But in 1504 Columbus made it back to Spain, where he died in 1506. He was probably convinced to his dying day that the lands he had explored were part of Asia. The single-mindedness that brought about the Enterprise of the Indies also prevented Columbus from appreciating the magnitude of what had resulted from his vision.

Chapter

3 Spices and Gold: Africa, India, and Asia

When King João II of Portugal sent Bartolomeu Dias out to sail around the southern tip of Africa, he was not putting all his eggs in one basket. The king's ultimate goal was trade with India and also, if possible, with the fabled Prester John, somewhere in Africa. To that end, he sent out another expedition in 1487, the same year that Dias left Portugal. This one was an overland journey undertaken by Pero da Covilhã and Afonso de Paiva. The two men were to go to Cairo together, then split up. Covilhã, who had been a spy for Portugal in both Spain and Morocco and who spoke Arabic fluently, was then to try to make his way to India. Paiva would head for Ethiopia in search of Prester John.

The two left Lisbon in the spring of 1487, crossed Spain to the coastal city of Barcelona, and boarded a ship that took them to Alexandria, by way of Naples and Rhodes. From there, they made their way to Cairo. At Cairo, probably disguising themselves as Muslims, they joined some Moorish merchants and sailed down the Red Sea to Aden. By now it was the spring of 1488. Paiva left the ship at this point and headed south for Ethiopia, intending to find Prester John and return to Portugal. In 1490 Covilhã found an Arab sailor willing to take him across the Arabian Sea to Calicut, on the southwest coast of India.

He spent some time traveling the west coast of India and learned a great deal about the spice trade of the Muslim merchants, who traded extensively between India and East Africa, including the Persian Gulf and Red Sea ports.

One of the things Covilhã learned was how the merchants used the weather to help them: "The traders took advantage of the monsoon wind, sending ships laden with spices, gems, and porcelains to Arab lands in February, and receiv[ing] their return cargoes in August and September."[33] To complete his researches, he went back across the sea to Ormuz, on the Persian Gulf, one of the great trading centers of the time. From there, he sailed south along the coast of East Africa to Sofala, in present-day Mozambique (21° S). From this journey, Covilhã learned about the trade in gold from the interior of Africa, and he satisfied himself that it was indeed possible to sail around Africa to reach India and Asia.

At this point, Covilhã decided it was time to report to King João, so he went back to Cairo. There he learned that Paiva had died, leaving no account of his travels. There he also met two Portuguese men whom King João had dispatched to find him. They told Covilhã that the king was more determined than ever to find Prester

40 ■ THE AGE OF EXPLORATION

John and that Covilhã himself must take over in Paiva's place. Before he left Cairo, however, Covilhã wrote a full report of his journey thus far and sent it back to Portugal with one of the king's agents. The other man accompanied him to Ormuz, where Covilhã disguised himself as a Muslim and went to Mecca. According to historian Boies Penrose:

> This perilous visit was not warranted in his instructions and can only be ascribed to [Covilhã's] love of adventure. Even this did not satiate his curiosity, for he went on to Medina, and thence to Mount Sinai, where in the Monastery of St. Catherine he heard his first Christian service in five years.[34]

Eventually, he made his way south to Ethiopia, the supposed realm of Prester John. He spent the remaining thirty years of his life there, "as a powerful and trusted (but probably captive) servant of the Emperor."[35] In 1520, more than thirty years later, a Portuguese ambassador, Rodrigo de Lima, arrived in Ethiopia and Covilhã, "by then an elderly, Africanized exile, was on hand to give assistance and to tell his life's story."[36]

Vasco da Gama

With Bartolomeu Dias back in Portugal after successfully rounding Africa and with Covilhã's report of the trade routes between East Africa and India, the stage was set for Portugal to begin a profitable India trade. João II of Portugal had died in 1495, and his twenty-six-year-old cousin Manuel became the new king. Manuel was determined to trade with India and began at once to ready a fleet for that purpose.

Bartolomeu Dias was hired to supervise the construction of the four ships in the fleet. Two were square-rigged ships, the flagship *São Gabriel* and the *São Raphael*, one was a lateen-rigged caravel called *Berrio*, and the fourth was a storeship. Many of the crew members had sailed with Dias around the cape. Dias, however, was not given command of this voyage; instead it went to Vasco da Gama, a gentleman of the Portuguese court. Not much is known of his

An illustration depicts the court of Prester John, a mythical Christian priest and king of Africa, whose legendary fame inspired King João II of Portugal to send an expedition in search of him.

background, but the fact that he was given command of such an important fleet over the more obvious choice, Dias, indicates that he was well respected and had considerable sea experience. In any case, the success of the mission justifies the choice in hindsight.

The fleet left Portugal's Tagus River on July 8, 1497, heading first for the Cape Verde Islands. They sailed southwest out into the mid-Atlantic in order to take advantage of prevailing winds. According to historian Boies Penrose, da Gama's voyage from the Cape Verdes to South Africa

Vasco da Gama, a gentleman of the Portuguese court, was appointed to lead an expedition with the objective of establishing a profitable trade between Portugal and India.

was far and away the greatest feat of navigation done up to that time. Columbus' passage from Gomera to the Bahamas was twenty-six hundred miles, sailed before a fair wind; in contrast da Gama's course was thirty-eight hundred miles [complicated by] . . . currents and contrary winds. Columbus took five weeks; da Gama three months. . . . Even da Gama's crews were conscious of their wonderful accomplishment; as they approached the shore [of the Bay of St. Helena, north of the cape] they put on their best clothes, fired off bombards, and dressed the ships with bunting.[37]

A few days later, they sailed on around the cape to Mossel Bay and stayed there for about two weeks. During that time, they broke up the storeship and reprovisioned the other three ships from it. They headed northeast again, and da Gama's chronicler noted, "we were then [December 16] already beyond the last discovery made by Bartolomeu Dias." On Christmas Day they sailed past a lovely section of coast that da Gama named Natal, in honor of Jesus' natal (birth) day, but they did not stop. They were beginning to have problems with the ships, however—a broken mast, a snapped mooring rope, and a lost anchor. The chronicler says:

> We now went so far out to sea, without touching any port, that drinking-water began to fail us, and our food had to be cooked with salt water. Our daily ration of water was reduced to a quartilho [about 1½ cups]. It thus became necessary to seek a port.[38]

On January 11 they anchored near a small river between the Limpopo River and Cape Correntes. The people who came to

Da Gama's fleet rounds the Cape of Good Hope off the southern coast of Africa. Da Gama learned a great deal about the African people during his travels.

meet them were friendly, and the explorers observed that there were more women than men. The Portuguese named the country Terra da Boa Gente (land of good people) and called the river Rio do Cobre (Copper River). They noted the use of copper and tin, both for ornaments and for weapons.

They continued north past the Zambezi to Quelimane, where they stayed for over a month. There they met another group of Africans and noted that "their lips are pierced in three places, and they wear in them bits of twisted tin." Many of the sailors suffered from an outbreak of scurvy in Quelimane, but they also got some good news from two men who came to visit them. These men were unimpressed with the goods the Portuguese had to offer. "A young man in their company—so we understood from their signs—had come from a distant country, and had already seen big ships like ours."[39] This indicated to the Portuguese that they were nearing their goal of reaching "the Indies."

Their next stop was Mozambique, a thriving Muslim port. The city dwellers were quite a change from the village natives that da Gama's crew had earlier encountered:

The people of this country . . . are Mohammedans [Muslims], and their language is the same as that of the Moors [that is, Arabic]. Their dresses are of fine linen or cotton stuffs, with variously colored stripes, and of rich and elaborate workmanship. They all wear *tocuas* [hats] with borders of silk embroidered in gold. They are merchants, and have transactions with white Moors [that is, Arabs], four of whose vessels were at the time in port, laden with gold, silver, cloves, pepper, ginger, and silver rings, as also with quantities of pearls, jewels, and rubies, all of which articles are used by the people of this country.

The Portuguese explorers were aided in Mozambique by the presence of a sailor

The People of Southern Africa

On Thursday, January 11, 1498, Vasco da Gama's crew anchored near a small river in southern Africa and went onshore in boats at Terra da Boa Gente and the Rio do Cobre. This account is from the unnamed crew member who wrote A Journal of the First Voyage of Vasco da Gama, *translated by E. G. Ravenstein.*

"This country seemed to us to be densely populated. There are many chiefs, and the number of women seems to be greater than that of the men, for among those who came to see us there were forty women to every twenty men. The houses are built of straw. The arms of the people include long bows and arrows and spears with iron blades. Copper seems to be plentiful, for the people wore [ornaments] of it on their legs and arms and in their twisted hair. Tin, likewise, is found in the country, for it is to be seen on the hilts of their daggers, the sheaths of which are made of ivory. Linen cloth is highly prized by the people, who were always willing to give large quantities of copper in exchange for shirts. They have large calabashes [gourds] in which they carry sea-water inland, where they pour it into pits, to obtain the salt [by evaporation]."

who had once been a prisoner of the Moors and had learned some Arabic. He served as a translator for da Gama and reported not only the presence of jewels and spices at ports farther north, but also "that Prester John resided not far from this place; that he held many cities along the coast, and that the inhabitants of those cities were great merchants and owned big ships."[40] On the strength of these reports, da Gama headed north with the aid of a local pilot, a sailor who was very familiar with the coast and its harbors. Pilots were extremely valuable to mariners sailing into unfamiliar harbors because of their thorough and specialized knowledge of local coastlines, including rocks, shoals, and other dangers.

On Saturday, April 7, 1498, they anchored off the city of Mombasa, in present-day Kenya. The residents of Mombasa were suspicious of the Portuguese. At one point, several men came out to the flagship *Gabriel* in the middle of the night and attempted to cut the ship loose. Da Gama's stay in Mombasa was short, but his next move was only a short distance up the coast to Malindi. There the reception was more cordial, and although da Gama at first refused to leave his ship, the local sultan came out to visit, wearing "a robe of damask trimmed with green satin," and "seated on two cushioned chairs of bronze, beneath a round sunshade of crimson satin attached to a pole."[41]

During the nine days they spent at Malindi, the crew was treated to "fêtes, sham-fights, and musical performances." Malindi reminded the Portuguese of Alcochete, a town on the bank of the Tagus River, near Lisbon: "Its houses are lofty and well whitewashed, and have many windows; on the landside are palm-groves, and all around it maize and vegetables are being cultivated."[42] Da Gama's greatest accomplishment in Malindi, however, was to secure the services of Ibn Majid, a native of Gujarat in western India who was one of the most experienced pilots of the Indian Ocean.

India at Last

With this able pilot on board, da Gama left Africa on April 24, 1498, headed for the city of Calicut on the southwestern coast of India, the same city Covilhã had visited in 1490. The trip was uneventful. A few days out from Malindi, da Gama's chronicler notes that "we once more saw the North Star, which we had not seen for a long time."[43] European sailors had for centuries counted on the North Star to determine their latitude, but it cannot be seen south

of about 9° N. This rather casual mention shows how far the Portuguese had come, both literally and figuratively, in the twenty-five years since they had first dared to cross the equator. They arrived in Calicut on May 20, finally fulfilling Henry the Navigator's great dream.

Unfortunately, not everyone at the busy port of Calicut was as happy to see the Europeans as the Europeans were to be in India. The Arabs and Persians had been trading with the merchants of Calicut for generations and had worked out a balance of power. Now the Portuguese were here, with an obviously well-funded and well-organized expedition, and looking like serious rivals. Da Gama and thirteen of his men were invited ashore to meet the local leader. First they were shown a Hindu temple, but the Portuguese were so convinced that the Indians were Christians that they persuaded themselves that they were seeing a church. They were shown a picture of the goddess Devaki, the mother of Krishna, and decided it was Mary, the mother of Jesus.

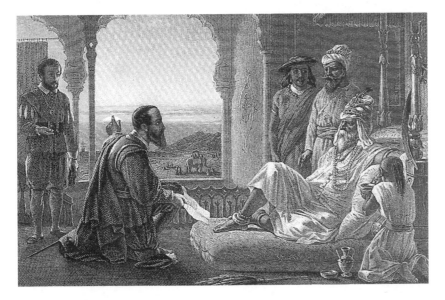

After finally fulfilling Henry the Navigator's dream of reaching India, da Gama meets with the local leader in Calicut in an unsuccessful attempt to establish trade with India.

"Many other saints were painted on the wall of the church," the chronicler says, "wearing crowns. They were painted variously, with teeth protruding an inch from the mouth, and four or five arms."[44]

Da Gama's visit ashore was neither happy nor profitable. He and his men were physically detained for several days and narrowly avoided an assassination attempt. Their attempts to sell their goods resulted in frustration. The local merchants were scornful of the merchandise the Portuguese had brought. Eventually, da Gama sent the crew members ashore

by twos and threes, taking with them bracelets, clothes, new shirts, and other articles, which they desired to sell. We did not, however, effect these

sales at the prices hoped for. . . . A very fine shirt which in Portugal fetches 300 reis, was worth here only two fanôes, which is equivalent only to 30 reis.[45]

In late August, after three months in Calicut, da Gama gave up attempting to trade and set sail for Portugal. It was not a pleasant journey. The trip across the Indian Ocean alone took three months because of storms and head winds, and many crew members died of scurvy. In January 1499 they finally made it back to Malindi, where they were able to buy oranges. Even more scurvy sufferers died, however, since by then they were too sick to benefit from the fresh citrus fruit. A few days later they anchored near Mombasa in a bay they had earlier named São Raphael, "where we set

Scurvy

Scurvy was one of the most common diseases of sailors on long voyages. It is caused by a lack of vitamin C in the diet. Vitamin C is found chiefly in fresh fruits and vegetables, items in short supply in those days before refrigeration. Sailors pretty much expected that they would suffer from scurvy at some time. Here is one personal description of the disease, quoted in John R. Hale's book The Age of Exploration.

"It rotted all my gums, which gave out a black and putrid blood. My thighs and lower legs were black and gangrenous, and I was forced to use my knife each day to cut into the flesh in order to release this black and foul blood. I also used my knife on my gums, which were livid [red and inflamed] and growing over my teeth. . . . When I had cut away this dead flesh and caused much black blood to flow, I rinsed my mouth and teeth with my urine [to disinfect], rubbing them very hard. . . . And the unfortunate thing was that I could not eat, desiring more to swallow than to chew. . . . Many of our people died of it every day, and saw bodies thrown into the sea constantly, three or four at a time. For the most part they died with no aid given them, expiring behind some case or chest, their eyes and the soles of their feet gnawed away by the rats."

Da Gama's journeys paved the way for the production of more detailed maps of Africa, like this sixteenth-century map that illustrates the sea route around Africa to India.

fire to the ship of that name, as it was impossible for us to navigate three vessels with the few hands that remained to us. The contents of this ship were transferred to the two other ships."[46] The rest of the trip was reasonably uneventful, although the two ships were separated during a storm. The *Berrio*, under Nicolas Coelho, reached the Tagus on July 10, 1499. Da Gama, in the *São Gabriel*, stopped first in the Cape Verde Islands, then in the Azores, where his brother Paulo died, probably sickened from scurvy. Da Gama arrived in Portugal in early September, two years and two months after leaving. Of his original crew of 170 men, only 44 survived.

Vasco da Gama was greeted with a triumphal procession through the streets of Lisbon, and King Manuel gloated in a letter to Ferdinand and Isabella of Spain that "henceforth all Christendom, in this part of Europe, shall be able to provide itself with these spices and precious stones."[47]

The rest of Europe was eager to find out exactly what da Gama's route had been and to figure out how they could get involved in trading with India. It was clear from da Gama's reports, however, that for Portugal to profit to the utmost, they would have to find a way to take control of the eastern trade from the Muslims who currently held it.

When Vasco da Gama returned to Portugal, exploration of the African coast was essentially finished. Although more detailed maps were still to come, the attention moved totally from exploration and discovery to commercial concerns. The Portuguese had irrevocably turned to the East and left most of the exploration of the western continents to Spain. But in the words of historian John R. Hale, "Da Gama's achievement in reaching India puts him in the first rank of explorers of all time. . . . [His journey] required a courage and skill of seamanship that were equal to those possessed by his remarkable contemporary, Christopher Columbus."[48]

The Portuguese wasted little time in capitalizing on da Gama's news. In March 1500 the first completely commercial voyage to India set sail from Portugal, led by Pedro Alvares Cabral, and containing, among others, the old sailor Bartolomeu Dias. This voyage maintained Dias's old scheme of sailing far out to the southwest before swinging back around Cape Horn, and on this occasion they sighted land—Mount Pascoal on the Brazilian coast. Historians still debate whether the discovery was purely accidental or whether Cabral suspected something was there; but in any case, he did not stop to explore the land. He did, however, send a ship back to Portugal with the news, which certainly pleased the king of Portugal. Since the king had persuaded the pope to move the Spanish-Portuguese demarcation line farther to the west, this new land fell within the Portuguese sphere of influence, a fact still evident today in the languages of South America: Portuguese is spoken in Brazil; Spanish, in the other countries.

Cabral crossed the South Atlantic toward Africa with difficulty. A terrible storm destroyed four of his ships, including the one carrying Bartolomeu Dias. Despite the storm, the survivors made good time

An illustration depicts the Portuguese taking possession of Brazil. The Portuguese claimed control of Brazil after Cabral first sighted the country during his voyage to India.

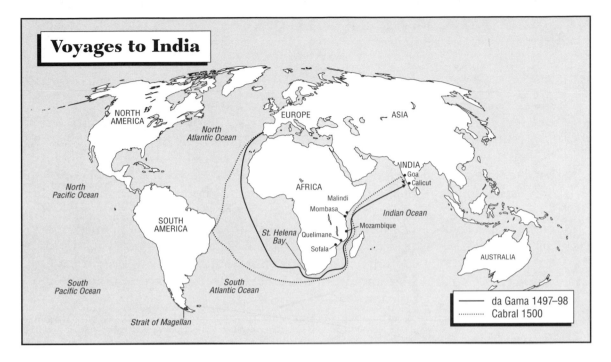

Voyages to India

Map labels: NORTH AMERICA, North Atlantic Ocean, EUROPE, ASIA, INDIA, Goa, Calicut, AFRICA, Malindi, Mombasa, Indian Ocean, Mozambique, North Pacific Ocean, SOUTH AMERICA, St. Helena Bay, Quelimane, Sofala, AUSTRALIA, South Pacific Ocean, South Atlantic Ocean, Strait of Magellan

Legend:
— da Gama 1497–98
········· Cabral 1500

and reached Goa in India after only six months. In Calicut, Cabral negotiated an agreement to build a factory—essentially a warehouse—onshore, but because he had offended local Muslim merchants, the residents stormed the factory and killed fifty of the Portuguese. Cabral responded full force, first burning ten Arab ships with their crews on board, and then bombarding the city of Calicut. Needless to say, this did not endear the Portuguese to the local rajah, and Cabral beat a hasty retreat to Cochin, in the south. There, according to historian Boies Penrose, "news of the warfare at Calicut had preceded them, and the local king, partly through fear of Portuguese artillery and partly through joy at the humbling of his more powerful neighbor, received the strangers cordially."[49]

Cabral, then, unlike da Gama, managed to leave India with a full cargo of spices and cloth. The news of his return was regarded by the established trading community of Venice as a disaster. In the words of one contemporary: "The worst news the Venetian Republic could have had."[50] The days of the Venetian monopoly of the India trade were over. On the way back, Cabral's crew visited Sofala, in East Africa, and planted his country's flag on the island of Madagascar.

King Manuel of Portugal was so enthusiastic about the results of Cabral's voyage that he began a practice of annual voyages between Portugal and India. What is more, he determined that the Portuguese would be a dominant presence in that area—and would not put up with any interference— and so sent out a large fleet headed by Vasco da Gama in 1502. Da Gama had been granted the title Admiral of India. He left Portugal with fifteen well-armed ships and was joined later by five more. Wasting no time, the Portuguese bombarded Calicut in retaliation for the destruction of the factory. The Portuguese knew that to profit

Spices

Samuel Eliot Morison explains why the Spice Islands were so sought after by Europeans for so long. This excerpt is from his book The European Discovery of America: The Southern Voyages, A.D. 1492–1616.

"And why were spices—especially clove, cinnamon, nutmeg, mace, and pepper—so avidly sought after in this era? They were part of life in both the European and Asiatic worlds. They flavored all kinds of cooked food. They were used in perfumes and (like myrrh) for embalming. Spices were among the most important ingredients of *materia medica* [medicines]. Before tea, coffee, and chocolate had been introduced to Europe, spices pepped up beer and wine, and in lieu of refrigeration they masked the unpleasant savor of decomposing food. Even today, how would you like to live without pepper, nutmeg, or cinnamon?"

from their monopoly of the route around Africa to India, they would have to destroy the Arab trade in spices. To do that, they used their superior gunnery.

King Manuel sent Afonso d'Albuquerque to India to become governor-general. Albuquerque established a base at Goa in 1511, as well as others on the Arabian coast at Ormuz and Socotra, and eventually took over the India trade. In 1513 a Portuguese ship sailed into Canton Harbor, "the first recorded European visit to China for more than a hundred and fifty years."[51] Also in 1513 the Portuguese reached the Moluccas and established a warehouse there for collecting the local spice—cloves. The Portuguese had achieved their goal of regular spice trade with the Indies.

4 Cartographers and Conquistadores: The Exploration of South and Central America

The years immediately after Columbus's first two voyages saw a flurry of activity in exploration, including two more voyages by the admiral and dozens of other voyages, led chiefly by Spanish seamen who had been with Columbus. These voyages were undertaken for a variety of motives, but mostly a combination of the famous trio: "gold, glory, and God." As time went on, those who went tended to be less explorers than conquistadores: conquerors. These were men who were heroic, courageous, and determined; at the same time, they were brutal, cruel, and treacherous. In the words of historian Boies Penrose, they "embodied much of the best and much of the worst of which the human soul is capable."[52] Nevertheless, they contributed greatly to European knowledge of this previously unknown landmass, its people, its plants and animals, and its geography.

Alonso de Ojeda was an adventurous young man who had sailed with Columbus on his second voyage. By all accounts, he was likable but completely unpredictable. Historian Samuel Eliot Morison says that Ojeda "was slim, handsome, and attractive alike to men and women—and also courageous, ruthless, greedy, and exceptionally cruel."[53] In 1499 he left Spain with three ships, financed by Seville merchants. He had with him two distinguished men: Juan de la Cosa—one of the great mapmakers and sailors of the time—and Amerigo Vespucci, a banker from Florence who had been living in Seville and working as an outfitter of ships.

Ojeda immediately began as he would continue: He disliked one of his caravels, so "he hijacked a better vessel, leaving the old one in exchange."[54] He continued in this way, helping himself to supplies and gear in Spain, Morocco, and the Canarics, before finally setting out across the Atlantic. Retracing the steps of Columbus's third voyage, completed not long before Ojeda left Spain, he went to Trinidad and the island of Margarita, off present-day Venezuela. He gathered a few pearls there but had trouble with the native Caribs and moved on. The Caribs, unlike the peaceful Taino of the northern islands, were not easily frightened by the Europeans and tended to fight back. Ojeda was not inclined, in any case, to peaceful means. According to one contemporary source, "He went along killing and robbing and fighting."[55]

He sailed on to the west, now entering territories previously unknown to Europe.

He came to one big island that he called Gijantes, because the natives seemed big to the relatively small Europeans. The island is present-day Curaçao. From there, the little fleet sailed into the Gulf of Maracaibo, where they saw a village built out over the water, just as the buildings are in low-lying Venice. They named the village Venezuela—"Little Venice"—and the name now applies to an entire country. Juan de la Cosa prepared a map in 1500 that shows in fairly accurate detail this part of what would later be known as the Spanish Main.

Ojeda then headed for Hispaniola to repair his ships and to stock up on food and water. Ojeda was not welcome in Hispaniola, as the other Spaniards there distrusted him, and he did not stay long. He stopped in the Bahamas and picked up some two hundred Taino to take back to Spain as slaves. This slave trade had been expressly forbidden by Queen Isabella, but Ojeda rightly guessed that no one would stop him. Some of the Taino died at sea, but the rest were sold in Cádiz.

Back in Spain, Ojeda somehow managed to stay in favor, despite his piracies and slave trading, and he was granted a new license to return to the Pearl Coast (near Margarita Island) to establish a trad-

Alonso de Ojeda, a ruthless Spanish conquistador, brutalizes the natives encountered on one of his expeditions to western territories previously unexplored by Europeans.

The Taino

In this selection from The Devastation of the Indies: A Brief Account, translated from the Spanish by Herma Briffault, Bartolomé de Las Casas describes the Taino, the Caribbean natives first met by Columbus and his crew. De Las Casas is speaking from fifty years' distance from the original encounter, although he himself later visited Hispaniola.

"And of all the infinite universe of humanity, these people are the most guileless, the most devoid of wickedness and duplicity [untruthfulness], the most obedient and faithful to their native masters and to the Spanish Christians whom they serve. They are by nature the most humble, patient, and peaceable, holding no grudges, free from embroilments [fighting], neither excitable nor quarrelsome. . . . They are also poor people, for they not only possess little but have no desire to possess worldly goods. For this reason they are not arrogant, embittered, or greedy. As to their dress, they are generally naked, with only their pudenda [genitals] covered somewhat. . . . They have no beds, but sleep on a kind of matting or else in a kind of suspended net called *hamacas* [hammocks]. They are very clean in their persons, with alert, intelligent minds, docile and open to doctrine, very apt to receive our holy Catholic faith, to be endowed with virtuous customs, and to behave in a godly fashion. And once they begin to hear the tidings of the Faith, they are so insistent on knowing more and on taking the sacraments of the Church . . . that truly, the missionaries who are here need to be endowed by God with great patience in order to cope with such eagerness."

ing post. He went but for unknown reasons decided not to create a post at or near Margarita. Instead, he went on past the Gulf of Maracaibo and attempted to establish a colony in present-day Colombia. There were no pearls and no gold, the local residents were unfriendly, and Ojeda's captains were fed up. They mutinied, put Ojeda in irons, and took him to Santo Domingo, where he was thrown into jail. His admirers in Spain eventually got him released, and Ojeda lay low for a few years.

Meanwhile, the cartographer Juan de la Cosa began to lead his own expeditions. He was one of the oldest of all of the explorers—in his fifties by this time—and was well-thought-of by most people, from common sailors to Queen Isabella. Shortly before her death, Isabella reportedly told another explorer, Cristóbal Guerra, "In navigation I command you to follow what appears best to Juan de la Cosa, for I know that he's a man who knows well what he is talking about when he gives advice."[56] In

Fed up with Ojeda after he led them on an unfruitful expedition to present-day Colombia, Ojeda's captains mutinied, put him in shackles (pictured), and had him thrown in jail.

1504 de la Cosa led an extremely profitable voyage to the Bay of Cartagena, during which his crew gathered pearls, gold, and slaves for resale in Spain.

The Isthmus

By 1508 Spain was thinking in terms of colonizing these new lands. In that year the new queen, Doña Juana, appointed two new governors: Alonso de Ojeda for the lands that are now the coast of Colombia and Diego de Nicuesa for the Isthmus of Panama and lands to the west. Nicuesa's settlement failed within months. Ojeda decided to settle in the harbor of Cartagena. There was immediate trouble when the settlers began raiding the interior for slaves. The Indians fought back with poisoned arrows and killed nearly a quarter of the Spaniards, including Juan de la Cosa, Columbus's old shipmate. Ojeda then moved the colony west to the Gulf of Urabá, where the situation was not much better. Ojeda was wounded but made his way back to Cuba on a passing ship, intending to send help back to the colony. Ojeda died a few years later in Santo Domingo.

After the departure of Ojeda, the leadership of the colony fell to Francisco Pizarro. Pizarro, who would later gain fame as the conqueror of the Incas, held things together until help arrived from Hispaniola in the person of Martin Fernandez de Enciso, the newly appointed governor. Enciso himself had little talent to motivate others, but he had brought with him a stowaway named Vasco Núñez de Balboa, who was a natural leader. Balboa moved the colony away from the area held by hostile South Americans to a spot on the other side of the Gulf of Urabá, which was named Darien. He got the settlers working together and sent ships to explore the coast, as well as parties inland to search for food and gold. Although he allowed his colonists to take slaves, Balboa generally got along with the natives, becoming a blood brother to one of the local caciques, or chiefs, and marrying his daughter.

From the natives, Balboa learned that the land was an isthmus and that beyond it lay another sea, even larger than the Atlantic. This information led Balboa to make an expedition across this fifty-mile stretch of very difficult terrain, a feat that is still impressive today. Balboa began on September 1, 1513, along with a party of several hundred natives and Spaniards, including Pizarro. They hacked their way through the tropical rain forest, swam across the numerous swamps and lakes, and fought several times with hostile bands.

On September 25, as the band approached the highest peak, Balboa, realizing that this was a great event, went on alone. The contemporary Spanish historian Herrera describes the occasion:

> [Balboa] . . . commanded his armie to halt, and himselfe went alone to the toppe, where, having sighted the *Mar del Sur* [South Sea], he knelt down, and raising his hands to Heaven, pouring forth mighty praises to God for His great grace in having made him the first man to discover and sight it. Having made this pious demonstration, he signalled all his people to come up, and they in their turn fell on their knees, rendering thanks to God for this great favor, while the Indians stood amazed at the rejoicing and ecstasy of the Castilians.[57]

Since the Spaniards' arrival hardly counted as a "discovery" as far as the natives were concerned, the "rejoicing and ecstasy" must have seemed very strange indeed. Four days later, Balboa and his party reached the shores of a bay that he named San Miguel, and Balboa waded into the water, sword raised high, and claimed the South Sea for Spain.

Balboa was not to have an opportunity to enjoy being a discoverer, however. Not long after he got back to Darien, Pedro Arias Dávila, usually known as Pedrarias, arrived to take his place as governor. Pedrárias came with a fleet of twenty ships and fifteen hundred men, including some who would later become famous, like Hernán de Soto and Bernal Díaz. Balboa was made *adelantado* [governor-general] of the South Seas and the provinces bordering it, and he spent the next few years exploring the isthmus and making plans to sail south to explore Peru. But he and Pedrarias did not get along, and they had very different ideas about how to deal with the local population. Pedrarias decided to rid himself of this annoyance.

So, one day in 1517, Vasco Núñez de Balboa, as kindly, loyal, and competent a conquistador as ever brought the

Vasco Núñez de Balboa led a fifty-mile expedition from the Gulf of Urabá across difficult terrain in search of a vast sea that was previously unknown except to natives.

cross and the banner of Castile over-seas, was seized by order of Pedrárias, tried, and condemned to death on the charge of treason and murder. Next day he and four companions were be-headed in the public square and their bodies thrown to the vultures.[58]

After Balboa's death, Pedrarias moved the colony from Antigua to Panama, found-ing in 1519 the oldest continuously exist-ing European settlement on the American mainland.

Rejoicing at his "discovery," Balboa wades into the water and proudly claims dominion of the South Sea for Spain.

Amerigo Vespucci and the Naming of Two Continents

On his voyage to Africa in 1500, Cabral had sighted Brazil and had sent a ship back to Portugal to report the news. The response was astonishingly speedy: when Cabral returned to the Cape Verde Islands in 1501, he found a mission already under way to explore this land. The commander of the small fleet of three caravels was Gonçalo Coelho, and on board was Amer-igo Vespucci, whose name would soon be-come attached to the newly discovered lands. On this voyage, they reached the coast of Brazil at its easternmost tip, about 5° S, and followed the coast south and southwest for more than two thousand miles. They certainly went beyond the mouth of the Rio de la Plata, possibly as far south as San Julian, in the part of present-day Argentina known as Patagonia. Since on his earlier voyage with Ojeda, Vespucci had seen much of the north coast of South America, from the mouth of the Orinoco to the Gulf of Maracaibo, he had himself been on voyages that "covered the greater part of the Atlantic coast of South Amer-ica, [and] revealed the continuity and vast size of that continent."[59] Vespucci wrote about these explorations and described them with some accuracy, which prompted the great cartographer Martin Wald-seemüller to suggest in 1507 that Vespuc-ci's name be given to the great southern continent. It was some years later, on maps of the world by Gerardus Mercator—another very influential mapmaker—that "America" was used for the northern conti-nent as well.

Vespucci was guilty of a bit of deceit; in his writings, he indicated that he had been on four voyages to the new lands, instead of only the two he had actually been on. He also falsified the dates of his voyages, indicating that he had traveled the coast of the continent in 1497, the year before Columbus's fourth voyage. Thus, Waldseemüller was taking Vespucci at his word when he added to his map the words "and the fourth part of the Globe, which, since Americus discovered it, may be called *Amerige,* or *Land of Americus,* or *America.*"[60] Most of the subsequent mapmakers and writers went along with Waldseemüller's suggestion, possibly feeling that the word itself fit nicely with the names of the other continents: Europe, Africa, Asia, America. The Spanish resisted the new name for centuries, preferring the term Las Indias. Because of this dispute over names, the Caribbean islands are still known as the West Indies. The one-time prevalence of the Spanish term also explains the use of "Indians" to identify all the indigenous peoples of the Americas.

The Aztecs

The Spanish continued to explore the mainland areas of America, first moving north from the Isthmus of Panama toward the Gulf of Honduras, the Yucatán, and the Gulf of Mexico. All through this area, there were a number of distinctly different groups of people. Some of the civilizations were very advanced, showing sophistication in techniques of pottery, weaving, metalworking, and building. Several of these peoples had elaborate systems for measuring time and making observations of the stars. They cultivated maize (corn), beans, and squash, and in some cases used irriga-

tion to improve crop production. What they did not have were iron tools, wheeled vehicles, or domesticated beasts of burden; and despite their position between two oceans, they were not shipbuilders or sailors. In at least two places, present-day Mexico and Peru, warlike tribes had set up vast organizations to force labor and other tribute from their neighbors.

The Aztecs in central Mexico were one of these warlike tribes. Their major city of Tenochtitlán, built on islands in Texcoco Lake, contained as many as three hundred

One of the warlike tribes encountered by the Spanish during their exploration and conquest of Mexico was the Aztecs, who are depicted here engaging in the ritual of human sacrifice.

thousand people. In addition, the Aztecs had expanded greatly to the west and south, taking over other tribes, and had possibly five million subjects. The Aztecs had buildings of stone and stucco; they had a strong oral tradition of history and poetry, as well as a system of picture writing. They had a centralized government that was stern and sometimes cruel; their powerful priesthood is known today largely for its human sacrifices. Few subjects were happy under Aztec domination, and the nearby independent city of Tlaxcala regarded the Aztecs with hatred.

Through contact with native people along the coast of Mexico, the Spanish had learned that there were more developed lands farther inland. With a view to better trading opportunities, Diego Velázquez, governor of Cuba, sent out a large fleet in 1519, headed by Hernán Cortés, to explore the inland and to trade, if possible. Cortés probably had visions of setting up a kingdom of his own right from the start. When he arrived on the mainland, he destroyed all of the party's ships, in order to prevent anyone from going back to Cuba. He then founded the town of Veracruz, had his officers elect some magistrates, resigned the commission he had received from Velázquez, and received from the magistrates a new commission.

The Conquest of Mexico

Having established himself as head of an independent command, Cortés made his way toward Tenochtitlán, stopping at various villages that were hostile to the Aztecs. In the process, he learned quite a bit about the military strengths and weaknesses of the Aztecs and their leader Montezuma (also spelled Moctezuma). Cortés's greatest alliance was with the town of Tlaxcala. The Tlaxcalans at first attacked the Spanish, but after Cortés defeated them in battle, they became allies and were instrumental in the defeat of the Aztecs. While the Spanish were staying in Tlaxcala, they met with ambassadors from Tenochtitlán. They brought presents and also threatened the Spanish, sending a message from Montezuma that said—according to Bernal Díaz, who had accompanied Cortés—"that he [Montezuma] should allow us to enter [the city], since once we were inside, he could kill us whenever he wished." Cortés was not alarmed by these words, and the Spanish, accompanied by a band of Tlaxcalans, made their way to Tenochtitlán in November 1519. As they approached the city, Díaz records,

> when we saw so many cities and villages built both in the water and on dry land, and this straight, level causeway, we couldn't restrain our admiration. . . . Some of our soldiers asked if what we saw was not a dream. . . . I do not know how to describe [it], since we were seeing things that had never before been heard of, or seen, or even dreamed about. . . . We didn't know what to say or whether it was real, with all the cities on the land and in the lake, the causeway with bridges one after the other, and before us the great city of Mexico. We were going there numbering less than four hundred soldiers. . . . What men have ever in the world shown such boldness?[61]

Díaz's amazement is understandable, for in 1519 Tenochtitlán was home to more people than lived at that time in Seville or

Cortés Meets the Aztecs

In a letter back to Spain, Hernán Cortés describes with amazement his first sight of one of Mexico's large cities. This excerpt is from Letters from Mexico, *translated and edited by A. R. Pagden.*

"The city is so big and so remarkable that, although there is much I could say of it which I shall omit, the little I will say is, I think, almost unbelievable, for the city is much larger than Granada [in Spain] and very much stronger, with as good buildings and many more people than Granada had when it was taken, and very much better supplied with the produce of the land, namely, bread, fowl and game and fresh-water fish and vegetables and other things they eat which are very good. There is in this city a market where each and every day upward of thirty thousand people come to buy and sell, without counting other trade; provisions as well as clothing and footwear. There is jewelry of gold and silver and precious stones and other ornaments of featherwork and all as well laid out as in any square or marketplace in the world. There is much pottery of many sorts and as good as the best in Spain. They sell a great deal of firewood and charcoal and medicinal and cooking herbs. There are establishments like barbers' where they have their hair washed and are shaved, and there are baths."

London. Cortés and his men entered the city and were greeted by the Aztecs. The chiefs "welcomed us in their language and made the sign of peace, touching the ground and with the same hand kissing the earth." Montezuma himself came out to meet Cortés, and Cortés "jumped from his horse and they showed great respect toward each other."[62] Cortés gave Montezuma a necklace, and through his interpreter—a young Indian woman the Spanish called Doña Marina—he made polite conversation with the Aztec king.

Montezuma was uncertain how to regard this visitor. According to Aztec tradition, the god of civilization, Quetzalcoatl, had been driven out of Mexico by hostile gods. The prophets said that he would return in the year One Reed and would come from across the water on white wings and appear as a white-skinned, bearded man. The year One Reed coincided with the European year 1519, the very year that the bearded, white-skinned Cortés arrived on Mexico's shores. Montezuma was uncertain whether Cortés was god or human, and he treated the Spaniard with caution.

Within days Cortés had taken Montezuma prisoner. He looted the town of its gold and silver, which he sent back to

Spain (although not all of it reached Spain; French pirates intercepted some of it). He spent the winter in Tenochtitlán, but in the spring he received word that a group of Spanish soldiers from Cuba had arrived on the coast to arrest him. Cortés left some of his men in the city and went with others to the coast, where he defeated the crew sent to arrest him. Many of those men joined Cortés and returned with him to Tenochtitlán, where the situation had turned ugly in his absence. The Spaniards left in charge had abused their power, and the Aztecs were in revolt. Cortés tried to

Montezuma

Bernal Díaz was with Cortés during the conquest of the Aztec Empire of Mexico. In this excerpt from The Bernal Diaz Chronicles: The True Story of the Conquest of Mexico, *translated and edited by Albert Idell, Díaz describes the great Aztec leader Montezuma.*

"The great Montezuma was about forty years old, of good height, well proportioned, and slender; he was not very dark, but of the color natural for an Indian. He did not wear his hair long, only long enough to cover his ears. He had few whiskers, dark and well set and sparse. His face was a little long, but pleasant, while his eyes were attractive, and he showed in his person and in his glance both affection and, when necessary, seriousness. He was most clean, bathing every day, in the afternoon. He had many women, daughters of lords, and he had two high chieftans' daughters for wives."

The great Aztec king Montezuma, whose downfall was hastened by his uncertainty about Spanish conqueror Hernán Cortés. Montezuma believed Cortés might be the Aztec god prophesied to return that year as a bearded, white-skinned man.

impose calm by bringing the captive Montezuma out to "speak to them [the Aztecs] from a roof top and tell them to stop the fighting and that we [the Spanish] wished to leave the city." Montezuma was reluctant to help but had little choice. When he went out to speak, however, "there was such a shower of stones and javelins that Montezuma was hit by three stones, one on the head, another on the arm, and the third on the leg."[63] Montezuma died from his wounds.

With Montezuma dead, Cortés had no hold over the Aztecs at all and decided to leave Tenochtitlán as quickly as he could. As Cortés and his followers fled over the causeway to the mainland, the Aztecs attacked fiercely, and the Europeans and their Tlaxcalan allies lost many men and horses. The survivors eventually managed to get to Tlaxcala, where they regrouped.

A year later, in the spring of 1521, the Spanish completed the conquest of Mexico. With fresh troops of both Spanish and Tlaxcalan warriors, Cortés laid siege to Tenochtitlán and this time completely defeated the Aztecs. The Spanish effectively trapped the Aztecs in their island city by cutting off water and food supplies from the mainland. As an added blow to the Aztecs, one of the Spanish soldiers from the first occupation had carried smallpox, a disease previously unknown in America. Lacking natural immunity, the Aztecs experienced a massive epidemic that killed many, further depleting both their numbers and their morale. The Spanish wasted no time in making their victory complete by means of harsh laws and physical destruction of important cultural symbols. They got rid of all vestiges of Aztec religion and monarchy, substituting representatives of the Catholic Church and the Spanish

Cortés fends off his Aztec attackers during the siege of Tenochtitlán, the success of which completed the Spanish conquest of Mexico.

court. Cortés then sent out men to explore the parts of Mexico and Central America the Spanish had not yet seen.

The Conquest of Peru

To the south of Mexico was another great American civilization. The Inca Empire in modern-day Ecuador and Peru had expanded greatly during the fourteenth and fifteenth centuries. It probably contained six to eight million inhabitants, governed

Spaniard Francisco Pizarro journeyed to Peru where he looted and brutally conquered the great Inca Empire, which was in the midst of a civil war.

by a supreme ruler known as the Inca. The Inca people were great engineers and builders. The Spanish had heard rumors of a great empire to the south, and Balboa had been planning to venture there shortly before his death. Francisco Pizarro, who had served under Balboa, was determined to find the empire and conquer it, thus gaining wealth and prestige for himself.

Pizarro made two failed attempts to reach Peru, one in 1524–1525 and the second in 1526. His successful expedition began in 1530, probably the worst possible time from the point of view of the Incas. In 1527 the great Inca leader Huayna Capac had died, probably of smallpox, for the diseases brought by the Spanish traveled faster across the land than did the Spanish themselves. Huayna Capac had not desig-

nated an heir, and the people divided into two factions—one in favor of Huayna's son Huáscar, the other in favor of his older, but illegitimate, son Atahualpa. Thus the Inca Empire was engaged in a bitter civil war at just the time that Pizarro arrived. Atahualpa had just defeated Huáscar's men in battle and set up camp in the mountain town of Cajamarca when he received word that the Spanish had arrived.

Pizarro led 62 cavalry and 106 infantry into the city of Cajamarca. There, like Cortés before him, he captured the monarch. A battle ensued, in which the Inca blunt clubs and quilted armor were no match for Spanish horses and guns and swords and armor of steel. Again, following the pattern set by Cortés, Pizarro kept Atahualpa captive for several months, while he looted the city of its gold and silver; once that was done, Pizarro had the king strangled and proceeded to move on to the capital city of Cuzco. The Incas were not so easily defeated as the Aztecs, but in 1532 they also fell. The Spaniards themselves quarreled over how to rule the Incas, and Pizarro was murdered by rivals in 1541. Civil wars continued, among the Incas and among rival Spanish groups, but the conquest was effectively complete by 1548, when Pedro de la Gasca became governor of Peru. By 1580 as many as six million Incas had died, mostly of smallpox and other diseases, but also from Spanish warfare.

How Cruel Were the Spanish?

Five hundred years after the Spanish conquest of Central and South America, it is customary to regard the Spanish as cruel conquerors who enslaved, tortured, and murdered the American Indians. Certainly the Spanish were guilty of many acts of brutality, but when they are judged by their motives and by the standards of the sixteenth century, rather than by those of the twenty-first century, a somewhat different story emerges.

In the sixteenth century, most Europeans accepted Aristotle's concept of "natural slavery." This was the idea that in every human society, there were some people who were born to serve others. Since European society was almost exclusively Christian, it is not surprising that the Spanish felt that it was the non-Christians of the world who might fill that slave class. Early in the days of Spanish colonization of the Americas, Queen Isabella of Castile "established the policy that Indians who accepted Christianity were free crown subjects. (Those who didn't could be sold into slavery.)"[64] In practice, even many of those who became Christians ended up working for Spanish masters in order to pay the royal tribute required of all crown

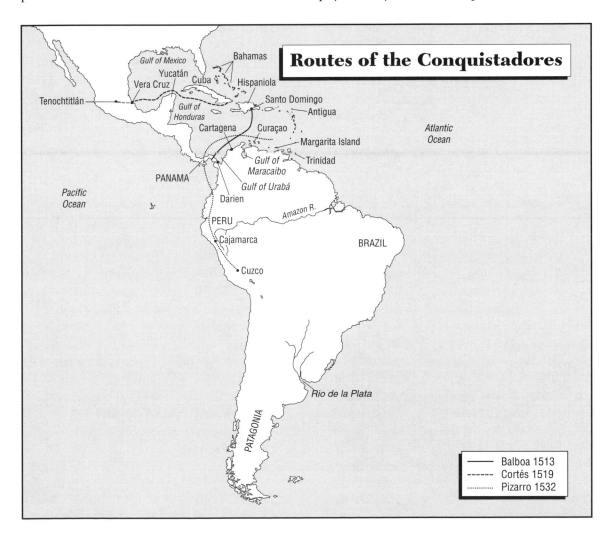

Routes of the Conquistadores

Gulf of Mexico
Bahamas
Yucatán
Cuba
Hispaniola
Vera Cruz
Santo Domingo
Tenochtitlán
Antigua
Gulf of Honduras
Cartagena
Curaçao
Margarita Island
Gulf of Maracaibo
Trinidad
PANAMA
Gulf of Urabá
Darien
Amazon R.
PERU
Cajamarca
BRAZIL
Cuzco
Pacific Ocean
Atlantic Ocean
PATAGONIA
Rio de la Plata

——— Balboa 1513
- - - - Cortés 1519
·········· Pizarro 1532

subjects. The conquistadores felt that in bringing their religion to the American Indians, they were bestowing a great gift. Often very pious and observant themselves, the conquistadores believed that baptism insured salvation; thus they held that any baptism, even baptism by force, was a good thing.

Officially, the Spanish colonists were under orders to treat native peoples fairly. This policy was embodied in the system known as *encomienda*, in which the crown allowed small landholders to use native labor, with the provision that they "take adequate care of Indians and instruct them in civilized behavior."[65] In practice, however, the *encomienda* did not always work that way. Many of the landholders—mostly ex-soldiers and other middle-class Spaniards who mainly wanted to get rich as quickly as possible—ignored the directives from Spain and treated their laborers as slaves.

Not every Spaniard went along with this brutality, however. In 1514 a Spanish priest named Bartolomé de Las Casas, who was himself a landholder and *encomendero* in Hispaniola, preached a sermon in which he denounced the Spanish treatment of the Indians. He then freed his own slaves

Are These Not Men?

In this selection, Bartolomé de Las Casas describes a sermon of the Dominican priest Antonio de Montesinos in December 1511. De Las Casas may have heard the sermon himself or only heard of it; in either case, it definitely influenced him in his campaign against Indian slavery in the West Indies. This translation by George Sanderlin is from Witness: The Writings of Bartolomé de Las Casas.

"Tell me, by what right or justice do you hold these Indians in such a cruel and horrible servitude? On what authority have you waged such detestable wars against these peoples, who dwelt quietly and peacefully on their own land? Wars in which you have destroyed such infinite numbers of them by homicides and slaughters never before heard of? Why do you keep them so oppressed and exhausted, without giving them enough to eat or curing them of the sicknesses they incur from the excessive labor you give them, and they die, or rather, you kill them, in order to extract and acquire gold every day?

"And what care do you take that they should be instructed in religion, so that they may know their God and creator, may be baptized, may hear Mass, and may keep Sundays and feast days? Are these not men? Do they not have rational souls? Are you not bound to love them as you love yourselves? Don't you understand this? Don't you feel this?"

Although many Spaniards treated the American Indians with viciousness and brutality, as Pizarro and his men are shown doing in this sixteenth-century illustration, not all of the Spanish colonists were guilty of such behavior.

and began a campaign to get better treatment for the natives that would last for the rest of his life. In 1552 he published a book called *The Devastation of the Indies* in which he told of Spanish atrocities and pleaded for the rights of the Indians.

Las Casas's account was entirely one-sided. He painted his countrymen as uniformly vicious, cruel, and wicked and the American Indians as uniformly "humble, patient, and peaceable, holding no grudges, free from embroilments [fights], neither excitable nor quarrelsome."[66] He ignored the role that disease played in the conquest. He also neglected to mention that Indians such as the Tlaxcalans had been instrumental in helping Cortés to defeat the Aztecs. Similarly, he ignored the historical profile of the Aztecs themselves: a conquering people who had enslaved and tortured many of the neighboring tribes of Mexico and practiced ritual human sacrifice.

Las Casas also ignored another reality: one of the reasons for the "disappearance" of the Indians of Central and South America was their intermarriage with the Spanish, creating a whole new race. In the words of Mexican poet Homero Aridjis, "The Spanish were conquered in turn by those they conquered." This combination of Spanish and Indian "blood and cultures created *la raza*—the new mestizo people who compose most of today's Latin America."[67] In contrast, the French, Dutch, and English who settled North America rarely intermarried with the natives of that continent. These Europeans, who systematically killed or drove off the original inhabitants of lands they wanted to settle, thus retained their ethnic heritage.

Chapter

5

The First Circumnavigation: Ferdinand Magellan and Juan Sebastián del Cano

By 1518—thanks to Columbus, Balboa, and many others—the general shape of the continent of South America, at least on the eastern coast, was clear. At this point, another foreigner arrived in the Spanish court who, like Columbus, was destined to bring fame to Spain. Fernão de Magalhães e Sousa, known to us as Ferdinand Magellan, was born in Portugal in about 1480. As a young man, he had traveled to India with a Portuguese delegation; he had been to the Malaysian port of Malacca; and he had probably been on a voyage of exploration eastward to the Moluccas. However, after about 1515 he was out of favor with the Portuguese court and saw no future for himself in that country. Therefore, like Columbus before him, he took himself to the Spanish court to present the details of his own great enterprise: sailing around South America to reach the East Indies.

The Line of Demarcation—
Again

Once again, the question of the line of demarcation between the Spanish and Portuguese lands came into question. According to the Treaty of Tordesillas, the line fell at the meridian of 46° W. Following that meridian through the poles to the other side of the world, this imaginary line would be at 180° minus 46°, or 134° E. No one knew exactly where the Spice Islands—the Moluccas—lay, but the Spanish naturally hoped that at least some of the islands fell into their sphere of influence. Since the Portuguese already had the monopoly on the route around Africa and since the Spanish had begun to explore South America, it only made sense to try to find a route to the East Indies through Spanish, rather than through Portuguese, territory. As it happens, the Moluccas fall well to the west (or Portuguese) side of the 134th meridian, but no one, least of all Magellan, knew this in 1518.

Magellan appeared before Charles I, king of Spain, in 1518 to present his plan. According to Bartolomé de Las Casas, who was present at the meeting, Magellan carried a globe and showed the court the route he intended to take, "except that he left the strait blank on purpose, so that no one would steal the knowledge of it from him."[68] Of course, he had no certain knowledge, only a guess about where a strait might be, but Europeans were eager to believe that it existed. Until Sir Francis Drake explored the coast of Tierra del Fuego in the 1570s, Europeans remained convinced that there was another large continental mass south of what would come to be called the Strait of Magellan. In 1616 Dutch sailors finally sailed around Cape Horn, the tip of South America, but the seas there were very stormy. Until the Panama Canal was built in the twentieth century, anyone sailing from Europe or the eastern coast of the Americas had to choose among the stormy Cape Horn route, the twisty and treacherous Strait of Magellan, or the long way east around Africa via the Cape of Good Hope.

Magellan apparently had little trouble convincing Charles to support his voyage, although the support may not have been completely wholehearted. As historian Boies Penrose says, "He was granted five ships, but they were very old and very patched-up, and one observer said that he would be afraid to sail even to the Canaries in them."[69]

The five ships were the *Trinidad*, commanded by Magellan; the *San Antonio*, commanded by Juan de Cartagena; the *Concepción*, commanded by Gaspar de Quesada, with Juan Sebastián del Cano as mate; the *Victoria*, commanded by Luis de Mendoza; and the *Santiago*, commanded by Juan Rodriguez de Serrano. Of the five ships, only three made it through the Strait of Magellan, and only one, the *Victoria*, completed the circumnavigation and made it back to Portugal.

Magellan and His Globe

Bartolomé de Las Casas had occasion to meet Ferdinand Magellan in Spain, in 1518, shortly after Magellan came there from Portugal. In this excerpt from Witness: The Writings of Bartolomé de Las Casas, *edited and translated by George Sanderlin, de Las Casas describes Magellan and the impression he made on the court of Charles V.*

"Magellan was carrying a well-painted globe, on which the whole world was depicted. On it he indicated the route he proposed to take, except that he left the strait blank on purpose, so that no one would steal the knowledge of it from him. . . . And when I spoke to Magellan and asked him what route he planned to take, he answered that he must go by way of Cape Santa Maria, which we call the Rio de la Plata, and from there sail up to the coast until he hit the strait.

'But suppose you do not find the strait by which you have to pass to the other sea?' I then asked.

He answered that if he did not find it, he would go by the route the Portuguese took. . . .

This Ferdinand Magellan must have been a man of spirit, valiant both in his thinking and in his undertaking of great things, although he did not have an imposing presence; for he was small in stature and did not seem to be much."

On August 10, 1519, there was an impressive departure ceremony at Seville, in which Magellan swore fidelity to King Charles, now known as Charles V, Holy Roman Emperor, who now ruled not only Spain but also most of central Europe and part of Italy. The five ships and their crews, totaling about 240 men, sailed downriver to San Lúcar, where they spent a month adding provisions for the journey. From there, they left on September 20, sailing to Tenerife, in the Canaries. One crew member, a Venetian gentleman named Antonio Pigafetta, kept a journal of the voyage in which he recorded that on Monday, October 3, 1519, "we took to the open Ocean Sea."[70]

Magellan began the voyage by sailing along the coast of Africa to Sierra Leone

Ferdinand Magellan (pictured) convinced King Charles I of Spain to support his plan of leading a voyage to the East Indies by sailing around South America.

(8° N latitude). From there, they sailed east to Brazil and traveled south along the coast of South America, occasionally stopping to trade with the natives. Magellan decided to spend the winter (from March until August) in San Julian Bay, in Patagonia (at 49° S). While they were there, Gaspar de Quesada and Juan de Cartagena led a mutiny against Magellan. These Spanish captains had never gotten along with their Portuguese commander, and the unrest came to a head during the long winter. Magellan and those who remained loyal to him managed to regain control of the fleet. Forty men were sentenced to death, but since the expedition could not afford to lose so many sailors, their sentences were commuted. Only Quesada and Luis de Mendoza were actually executed, although Cartagena and a French priest were sentenced to be marooned. Shortly before the fleet left San Julian, the two men were put ashore on an island with some food and drink. They were never heard from again. Juan Sebastián del Cano, the man who would eventually complete the circumnavigation, was one of the mutineers whose death sentence was commuted, and "as the voyage continued and he gave a good account of himself, Magellan appeared to forget or forgive his offense."[71]

The Strait

Magellan was no doubt happy to leave port when better weather arrived in late August, and the fleet moved farther down the coast, where they found a river and spent some time collecting fresh water, wood, and fish. During this time, Pigafetta tells

The Thing Seemed Almost Impossible

Maximilian of Transylvania was a secretary to Charles V, Holy Roman emperor. Here he describes Magellan's plan to sail westward to the Moluccas. The excerpt is from Magellan's Voyage Around the World: Three Contemporary Accounts, *translated and edited by Charles Nowell.*

"Their course would be this, to sail westward, coasting the southern hemisphere [till they came] to the East. The thing seemed almost impossible and useless, not because it was thought a difficult thing to go from the west right to the east . . . but because it was uncertain whether . . . nature, which has done nothing without the greatest foresight, had not so dissevered [cut off] the east from the west, partly by sea and partly by land, as to make it impossible to arrive there by either land or sea travelling. For it had not then been discovered whether that great region which is called Terra Firma [the landmass of North and South America] did separate the western sea from the eastern; it was clear enough that that continent, in its southern part, trended southwards. . . . For which reason it seemed . . . that these men were promising a thing from which much was to be hoped, but still of great difficulty."

us, the smallest ship in the fleet, the *Santiago* "was wrecked in an expedition made to explore the coast. All the men were saved as by a miracle, not even getting wet."[72] In late October, they discovered what might be the entrance to a strait.

Magellan sent two of the ships, the *San Antonio* and the *Concepción*, to explore the passage, while at first the *Trinidad* and the *Victoria* waited. The fleet was plagued with bad weather and storms, and they spent many days exploring various bays and inlets, trying to discover whether this strait went all the way to the ocean on the other side. Some time, as well, was spent fruitlessly waiting for the *San Antonio*, which had slipped away from the others and returned to Spain. Finally, on November 28, 1520, the depleted fleet came out of the strait into the Pacific Ocean.

Crossing the Pacific

At this point began the most tedious part of the journey—the voyage across the Pacific. Pigafetta tells us that the crew was "three months and twenty days without getting any kind of fresh food."[73] They were reduced to eating shipboard rats and boiling oxhides for their small nutritional value. Naturally there were no fresh fruits or vegetables, and nineteen

Magellan discovers the strait on the southern tip of South America that would later be called the Strait of Magellan. Although the strait offered an alternative to the stormy Cape Horn route, it was twisty and often difficult to navigate.

men died of scurvy, complicated by starvation. Magellan sailed north along the coast of South America for nearly a thousand miles before heading west. According to historian Boies Penrose, this procedure

> had both advantages and disadvantages. It took him up to the belt of the favorable trade winds, which made his ocean crossing the speedier, but it resulted in his course being to the northward of the Pacific archipelagoes, which would have provided much-needed refreshment for his scurvy-ridden crews.[74]

Historians Samuel Eliot Morison and Alan Villiers, themselves both sailors, believe that Magellan took the best possible course:

> Further south he would have run into hundreds of islands and atolls, each a coral-baited trap for European ships. Semi-starvation and scurvy were bad, but better than running aground and being stripped bare by nimble Polynesians. He could hardly have shaped a better course if he had had modern sailing directions, not only avoiding dangerous, island-studded waters but making best use of prevailing winds and currents.[75]

In any case, as Pigafetta tells us, their passage was calm and storm free. He says, "In truth it [the Pacific Ocean] is very pacific, for during that time we did not suffer any storm." They also encountered no land except for two deserted islands they named the Unfortunate Isles. Pigafetta takes note of the difference in the constellations in the southern hemisphere and describes the Southern Cross: "When we were in the midst of that open expanse, we saw a cross with five extremely bright stars straight toward the west, those stars being exactly placed with regard to one another."[76]

Landfall

Finally, on March 6, 1521, the little fleet reached a large island flanked by two smaller islands. Magellan wanted to stop at the larger island, Guam, and get fresh food, but Pigafetta tells us:

> He was unable to do so because the inhabitants of that island entered the ships and stole whatever they could lay their hands on. . . . The men were about to strike the sails so that we could go ashore, but the natives very deftly stole from us the small boat that was fastened to the poop of the flagship.[77]

As a consequence, Magellan spent very little time on Guam, but he named the island group the Ladrones (thieves) because of his experience there.

From Guam, Magellan moved on to the island group that would later be named the Philippines, after Philip II of Spain. The fleet first landed at the island of Homonhon, a small island in Leyte Gulf, where Magellan "had two tents set up on the shore for the sick and had a sow killed for them." On March 18, nine islanders approached the sailors and Magellan, "seeing that they were reasonable men, ordered food to be set before them, and gave them red caps, mirrors, combs, bells, ivory, bocasine [a fine linen cloth], and other things."[78] In return, the natives presented the Europeans with fish, arrack (a potent fermented drink), bananas (which were new to Pigafetta), and coconuts. Pigafetta was quite impressed with the many uses the people made of coconuts and coconut palms, and all the crew members felt that these islanders were much more civilized than those in the Ladrones.

Magellan had brought along on the voyage a slave he called Enrique de Malacca, a native Malaysian. He had bought Enrique during his visit there with a Portuguese voyage in 1511. On March 28, 1521, Enrique, speaking in his native language, hailed eight men in a small boat that was approaching Magellan's ship. The delegation "immediately understood him [and] came alongside the ship."[79] If Enrique had indeed been born in the Moluccas, at about 130° E longitude, he had now completely circumnavigated the globe. Likewise, if Magellan, as seems likely, had gotten as far east in 1511 as the longitude of the Philippines, he had also covered 360° of longitude, although not in the same voyage or in the same direction. It is likely that one of these two men was the first to have been all the way around the world. It was left to other members of Magellan's crew to complete the east-to-west circumnavigation, however, for neither the leader of the expedition nor his slave would leave the Philippines.

Magellan's journeys through the strait and across the Pacific Ocean were long, difficult, and often treacherous. Of the five ships and 240 crew members that began the journey, only one ship and 35 survivors made it back to Spain.

The Death of Magellan

The sailors then moved on to investigate the other islands of the group. At Cebu, Magellan entered an alliance with a local king. At first all went well. The two leaders gave one another gifts and held parties and festivals for their people. The islanders observed Magellan and his crew celebrating Mass, and some, including the king, expressed a desire to become Christians. Pigafetta says that Magellan "told them that they should not become Christians for fear or to please us, but of their own free wills." It is unlikely that they knew much about Christianity from Magellan's brief explanations. Magellan, though sincere enough in his own beliefs, knew his own limitations

and offered to bring priests and friars to teach the faith. He also told them that "if they became Christians, he would leave a suit of armor,"[80] and this was apparently of great interest to the islanders.

A few days later, the king told Magellan that he still wanted to become a Christian, but that not all of his chiefs did. Magellan had the chiefs called together and made it clear to them where the strength and firepower of Spain stood on the matter:

> [Magellan] told them that, unless they obeyed the king as their king, he would have them killed and would give their possessions to the king. They replied that they would obey him. The captain told the king that he was going to Spain, but that he would return again with so many forces that he would

make him the greatest king of those regions, as he had been the first to express a determination to become a Christian.[81]

So the king was baptized and renamed Don Carlo, after the Emperor Charles V; his son was named Don Fernando, after the emperor's brother. Altogether, Pigafetta says, five hundred men were baptized, and later the queen and some three hundred women and children.

Now Magellan wanted to show the might of Spain and the value of being its ally. Mactan, the neighboring island of Cebu, had two chiefs, one of whom was loyal to the king of Cebu. This chief approached Magellan and asked for help in fighting the other chief, and Magellan responded at once, apparently believing this would cement the power of the now-Christian king. Magellan took three boatloads of men, followed by several boatloads of men from Cebu, across the strait between the two islands. He did not take advantage of the opportunity for a surprise attack, but rather sent a message ashore that if the natives would obey the king of Spain and recognize the Christian king of

Hardships at Sea

Antonio Pigafetta, in this contemporary account of Magellan's voyage, describes the long journey across the Pacific and the difficulties the crew endured, including food shortages and scurvy. This excerpt is from Magellan's Voyage Around the World: Three Contemporary Accounts, *translated and edited by Charles Nowell.*

"Wednesday, November 28, 1520, we debouched [exited] from that strait, engulfing ourselves in the Pacific Sea. We were three months and twenty days without getting any kind of fresh food. We ate biscuit [dry crackers], which was no longer biscuit, but powder of biscuits swarming with worms, for they had eaten the good. It stank strongly of the urine of rats. We drank yellow water that had been putrid for many days. We also ate some ox hides that covered the top of the mainyard [rope] to prevent the yard from chafing the shrouds [sails], and which had become exceedingly hard because of the sun, rain, and wind. We left them in the sea for four or five days, and then placed them for a few moments on top of the embers, and so ate them; and often we ate sawdust from boards. Rats were sold for one-half ducado [a lot of money, by sailors' standards] apiece, and even then we could not get them. But above all the other misfortunes the following was the worst. The gums of both the lower and upper teeth of some of our men swelled, so that they could not eat under any circumstances and therefore died."

Cebu as their leader, all would be well; otherwise, "they should wait to see how our lances wounded." By the time Magellan's landing party of fifty men came ashore on the morning of April 27, 1521, they were faced by an organized army of fifteen hundred. The Spanish muskets and crossbows proved useless: the range was too great for the muskets, and the defenders' wooden shields diverted the crossbow bolts. Magellan's ships were anchored out at sea, but too far away for their cannons to be of any help. The islanders attacked ceaselessly with iron-tipped bamboo spears, arrows, and pointed stakes. Pigafetta was among the men who went onshore and saw Magellan die. Magellan was wounded and fell facedown, "when immediately they rushed upon him with iron and bamboo spears and with their cutlasses, until they killed our mirror, our light, our comfort, and our true guide."[82] The remaining Europeans fought their way back to the boats and escaped to Cebu. Of the fifty who went ashore, eight besides Magellan were killed.

The Circumnavigation Completed

After Magellan's death, things fell apart badly for the Spanish. The remaining crew members chose two new commanders, Duarte Barbosa and Juan Rodriguez de Serrano, but they enjoyed that status for only a few days. Enrique, Magellan's slave, took to his bed with an injury after the battle and announced that since his master was dead, he was now a freeman. Barbosa threatened Enrique with a flogging if he did not get up and get to work, and En-

rique retaliated by going to the Christian king and proposing a plot to hijack the Spanish ships and merchandise. The king accordingly invited the Spanish commanders to a dinner, with the promise of giving them some jewels for the king of Spain. Twenty-five men went, including Barbosa and Serrano, and all were killed. Nothing more is known of the fate of Enrique.

The remaining men on board the ships—including Pigafetta, who had suffered a poison-arrow injury in the battle at Mactan—weighed anchor when they saw the commotion onshore and attempted to help by shelling the city. Eventually they left Cebu and made for the island of Bohol, where they took stock of their situation. Of the three remaining ships, the *Concepción* was in the worst shape, and they did not have enough men to sail three ships in any case. So they scrapped the *Concepción* and divided her men and her stores between the *Trinidad* and the *Victoria*. Juan Carvalho was chosen captain-general of the much-reduced fleet, Gonzalo Gómez de Espinosa became captain of the *Trinidad* and Juan Sebastián del Cano became captain of the *Victoria*.

The two ships made their way around the islands of the Pacific. First they went to Quipit, on Mindanao, then west to Palawan and Borneo, where they were quite impressed with the sultan of Brunei. From Brunei, they sailed back east to the southern coast of Mindanao, where they got directions to the Moluccas. Finally, on November 6, 1521, they reached Tidore, in the long-sought Spice Islands. As Pigafetta says:

> The pilot who still remained with us told us that those four islands were Molucca. Therefore, we thanked God and as an expression of our joy dis-

Magellan is attacked and killed by natives on the Philippine island of Mactan. The ambush occurred after Magellan agreed to help the natives from the neighboring island of Cebu, who were warring with the Mactan islanders.

charged all our artillery. It was no wonder that we were so glad, for we had passed twenty-seven months less two days in our search for Molucca.[83]

Twenty-nine years after Columbus set out to do it, Europeans had actually sailed west to reach the fabled Spice Islands.

At Tidore, both ships traded for cargoes of cloves and decided it was time to head back to Spain. In order to increase their chances of getting home with this valuable cargo, the captains decided to split up: *Victoria*, under del Cano, would take forty-seven of the original crew and thirteen Indonesians and go by way of the Cape of Good Hope. *Trinidad*, meanwhile, under Espinosa, would take the remaining fifty-three crew members and sail back across the Pacific to Panama, where they hoped to find Spaniards who would help them transport their goods across the isthmus and get them on a ship bound for Spain.

The *Trinidad*'s plans did not work out, however. First, they stayed at Tidore for three months, making repairs to the ship. When they finally left, they had constant easterly winds and stormy weather, and by the time Espinosa had turned the ship around and sailed back to the Moluccas,

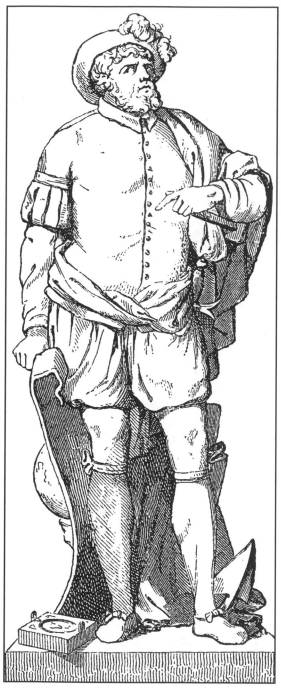

After Magellan's death, Juan Sebastián del Cano became captain of the Victoria, *the only ship from Magellan's fleet to complete the first circumnavigation of the globe and make it back to Spain.*

over half of his crew had died. While they were away from Tidore, a Portuguese fleet had arrived to reestablish control of the area. The *Trinidad* and her crew were captured by the Portuguese, who took the cargo and goods for their own profit and imprisoned the men. Eventually, four of the men, including Espinosa, made it back to Spain, but most died in the Indies.

Meanwhile, the *Victoria* headed for Africa across the Indian Ocean. Del Cano wisely decided not to stop at Bali, Java, or Sumatra, since the Portuguese would likely be there, and his crew might have ended up like Espinosa's. But it was a long way without landing, and the crew was miserable, cold, sick, and hungry by the time they reached Africa. Pigafetta says that some of the men wished to stop at Mozambique, even though they knew it to be a Portuguese settlement,

> because of the severe cold, and especially because we had no other food than rice and water; for as we had no salt, our provisions of meat had putrefied. Some of the others however, more desirous of their honor than of their own life, determined to go to Spain living or dead.[84]

And so they did, although more died than lived. On July 9, they reached the island of Santiago in the Cape Verdes. Because the Portuguese controlled the Cape Verdes, del Cano told his shore party to claim that they had lost their way coming back from the Caribbean. This deception worked long enough for the Spanish to get some rice, but a few days later the Portuguese got suspicious and del Cano beat a hasty retreat, leaving thirteen men as prisoners of the Portuguese. When the crew of the *Victoria* got the rice, they asked the Portuguese what day it was and were amazed to be told that it was Thursday, "for it was Wednesday with us, and we could not see how we had made a mistake."[85] They had not made a mistake, of course, but only crossed the international date line—which is to say, they had gained twenty-four hours by sailing continually west. This unexpected consequence of their voyage continued to puzzle them, however, until they returned to Spain and an astronomer explained it to them.

Sailing with a much-reduced crew of eighteen Europeans and three Indonesians, del Cano reached San Lúcar on September 6, 1522, and sailed up the river to Seville, arriving on September 8. Del Cano was greeted graciously by the emperor and given, in addition to back wages and an annual pension, a new coat of arms—which included cinnamon sticks, cloves, and nutmeg, along with a globe bearing the motto "*Primus circumdedisti me*" ("You first circum-

navigated me"). The emperor agreed to negotiate for the release of the thirteen sailors held captive in the Cape Verdes and this was done. These thirty-one, plus the four from the *Trinidad* who made it back to Spain a few years later, were the only survivors of the circumnavigation.

What It All Meant

Magellan and del Cano together made a tremendous contribution to geography and to science in general. If there was anyone left who believed that the earth was flat, the voyage demonstrated its spherical nature once and for all. It certainly demonstrated that, in direct opposition to traditional theory, there is far more water than land on the globe. It established firmly the distance around the earth and the relative positions of the major continents.

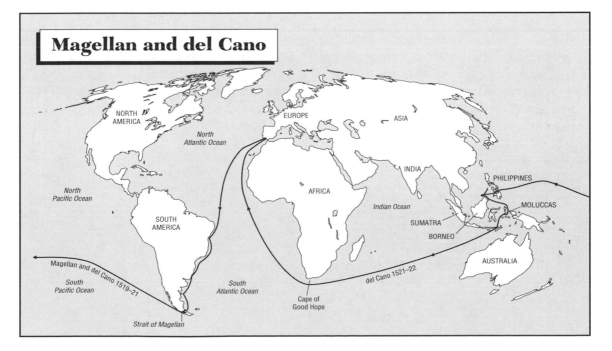

Magellan and del Cano

NORTH AMERICA
North Atlantic Ocean
North Pacific Ocean
SOUTH AMERICA
South Pacific Ocean
Magellan and del Cano 1519–21
Strait of Magellan
South Atlantic Ocean
EUROPE
AFRICA
Cape of Good Hope
ASIA
INDIA
Indian Ocean
SUMATRA
BORNEO
PHILIPPINES
MOLUCCAS
del Cano 1521–22
AUSTRALIA

A triumphant procession is held in Seville, Spain, to honor the arrival of del Cano and the remaining crew of the Victoria. *Despite the huge loss of life, the ultimately successful expedition made invaluable contributions to science.*

Although the voyage accomplished Magellan's intention of showing that the East Indies could be reached by sailing across the Pacific, it proved perhaps primarily that this was not a practical way to go. It took far too long, for one thing, and the *Trinidad*'s experience showed the great difficulties involved in sailing eastward back to the Americas or Europe. Still, the commercial possibilities were worth going after. The sale of the cloves and other spices from the *Victoria*'s cargo more than paid for the entire voyage. After a few more Spanish ships sailed west but failed to return, Charles V sold his interests in the Moluccas to Portugal. The Spanish were in any case busily occupied in the Americas. Spanish activity in the Pacific never completely stopped, however, and in 1565 they successfully colonized the Philippines. Also in the same year, a Spaniard named Andrés de Urdaneta determined to find a route from the Philippines back to Mexico, "and accomplished the feat by sailing boldly into a high latitude and crossing the Pacific in a wide northern arc, which took him at least to the forty-second parallel."[86] Since the Spanish were firmly established in Mexico, their trade with the Philippines and other Pacific islands was routed through that settlement from that time on.

6 The Exploration of North America

The story of the exploration and conquest of the southern continent is extremely well documented. The Spanish conquistadores often left multiple eyewitness accounts of their exploits. Even Magellan's hazardous voyage left two first-person accounts. Unfortunately for historians of today, accounts of the exploration of North America are not so plentiful. The explorers of North America had a more difficult time of it than did those in the south. The weather was much worse, for one thing. For another, the heavily forested eastern shores offered few water routes to the interior, making inland exploration difficult. What is more, it was not so profitable, since there were no equivalents to the Pearl Coast and no wealthy empires to loot for gold and silver. Still, during the sixteenth century, mariners of several European nationalities mapped the entire eastern coast of the continent, the Spanish explored the Gulf region and much of the Southwest, as far inland as Oklahoma and Kansas, and the French made their place in the Saint Lawrence Valley.

John Cabot

Adventurers from the northern reaches of Europe had explored the North Atlantic for centuries; some are believed to have seen the shores of North America. The Norsemen had settled Greenland in the tenth century and had set up a short-lived colony in a place they called Vinland in the thirteenth century. This was probably in present-day Newfoundland. Both the Greenland and Vinland colonies had died out by the middle of the fourteenth century and were so thoroughly "forgotten by southern Europe . . . that when a Portuguese from the Azores made Cape Farewell [Greenland] in 1500, it was mapped as a new discovery and given a new name."[87]

Not long after Columbus made his momentous first voyage, England got into the exploration game by hiring a sailor called John Cabot to explore the northern reaches of the Atlantic and to look for a northern passage to the Indies. Little is known about Cabot, and neither he nor any of his crew left a firsthand account of either of his voyages. Cabot himself was Italian— his name was probably originally Caboto or Chiabotto. He became a naturalized citizen of the city-state of Venice in 1476 and somehow ended up in England by 1495. In January 1496 the Spanish ambassador in England wrote to King Ferdinand that "a man like Columbus" had proposed to King Henry VII "another business like that of the Indies."[88]

King Henry VII (pictured), desirous of increasing England's power in Europe, was quick to grant John Cabot a patent to discover lands on behalf of England.

Henry VII was eager to expand England's place in Europe, and in March 1496 he granted Cabot a patent for discovery. This took the form of a letter, which gave Cabot and his sons Lewis, Sebastian, and Santius these rights:

> Full and free authoritie, leave, and power, to sayle to all partes, countreys, and seas, of the East, of the West, and of the North, under our banners and ensignes [flags], with five ships . . . and as many mariners or men as they will have with them in the saide ships . . . to seeke out, discover, and find, whatsoever iles, countreys, regions or provinces of the heathen and infidelles, whatsoever they be, and in what part of the world soever they be, whiche before this time have beene unknowen to all Christians.[89]

Cabot left Bristol, England, in May 1497. Unlike most of the Spanish and Portuguese explorations, his was a small expedition. He had only one ship, the *Mathew*, which was probably about the same size as Columbus's *Niña*. His crew was small as well: only eighteen men, plus Cabot's young son Sebastian, who would later become famous as an explorer in his own right. The expedition was gone from England for three months, and they certainly found land, but historians have still not determined exactly which land. Historian Samuel Eliot Morison, who is himself a sailor, believes that Cabot covered the entire eastern coast of the island of Newfoundland, from Cape Bauld on the north to Cape Race on the south, but that he did not see the mainland of Canada or Cape Breton Island, off the coast of Nova Scotia. Other historians disagree and claim that Cabot landed at Nova Scotia, or at least on Cape Breton, going through the strait that was later named after him. In any case, Cabot was back in England in August, making a presentation to King Henry VII.

Cabot apparently thought he had reached Asia—but not the habitable parts of that continent; those, he guessed, must be farther south. He must have convinced Henry that the land he had found was something previously unknown, for "the royal household books record that on 10–11 August 1497 the king gave £10 'to hym that founde the new Isle.'"[90] Six months later, Cabot was getting ready to go back. On February 3, 1498, Henry VII issued a new patent to Cabot, this one giving him six ships and the right to enlist sailors, "and theym convey and lede to the lande and Iles of late founde by the seid John in oure name."[91] Cabot fitted out five ships with provisions and with items for trading, and left Bristol in early May 1498. One of the ships had trouble and stopped in Ireland. The other four were never heard from again. Polydore Vergil, an English historian of the time, wrote lightly of Cabot that he "found his new lands only in the ocean's bottom, to which he and his ship are thought to have sunk, since, after that voyage, he was never heard of more."[92]

The Role of Portugal and England

Not long after Cabot's voyages, a Portuguese farmer named João Fernandes decided to try his luck in northern waters. He had been living in the Azores but had visited England. In 1499 he received permission from King Manuel of Portugal "to go in search of and discover certain Islands of our sphere of influence."[93] Although he may have considered finding a northwestern route to the Indies, the letter from King Manuel makes it clear that the main purpose of the voyage was to find an island or islands. Historian Samuel Eliot Morison says that it is likely that King Manuel, "having heard of John Cabot's discovery of Newfoundland, and believing that it lay on the Portuguese side of the Line of Demarcation, wished to forestall the English by settling the New Isle. From his point of view, the English had no proper title to it."[94] In any case, Fernandes and his crew

An illustration depicts Cabot's discovery of land in North America, which he believed to be an unknown part of Asia. To this day, historians disagree about whether Cabot landed at Nova Scotia or the island of Newfoundland.

found land, probably Greenland, which had been forgotten in the years since the disappearance of the Norse settlement. On a 1527 map, Greenland is marked with the notation "Because he who gave the *aviso* [the "land, ho!"] was a *labrador* [farmer] of the Azores, they gave it that name."[95] By the seventeenth century, the name Labrador had moved to the eastern part of the Canadian mainland.

Before Fernandes returned from the icy northern waters, King Manuel had given a similar grant for exploration to another Portuguese sailor, Gaspar Corte-Real. Corte-Real went on two voyages to the regions around Newfoundland and, possibly, Greenland, in 1500 and 1501. On his second voyage, he sent two ships back to Lisbon and continued sailing south to explore. He was never heard from again. In 1502 his brother Miguel set out to explore the same area; he, too, was lost, though one of his ships managed to return.

Much of what historians know about Sebastian Cabot comes from Cabot himself, told in his old age. He was always good at putting himself in the best possible light, and his stories were sometimes contradictory. In later life, he claimed that in 1509 he made an attempt to discover the Northwest Passage to China, and some historians accept that he went as far as 67° N latitude and possibly even went into Hudson Bay. Others, like Samuel Eliot Morison, place the 1509 voyage "in the doubtful class."[96] In 1521 a group of London merchants turned down a proposal by Cabot to provide him with five ships to sail to Newfoundland. Among other reasons they gave, they commented that Sebastian, "as we hearsay, was never in that land hym self, all [even] if he makes reporte of many things as he hath heard his Father and other men speke in

tymes past."[97] Whether or not Sebastian Cabot made any of these earlier voyages, he certainly sailed for the Spanish Crown in 1525–1528 and explored the region of the Rio de la Plata.

Others continued to explore the northern coast of the continent during the first half of the 1500s. In 1520 the Portuguese João Alvares Fagundes sailed up the Saint Lawrence River and explored the Bay of Fundy. He attempted to set up a settlement at Cape Breton, but it failed. Jean Alfonce, his chief pilot on a later voyage, remarked about Cape Breton Island that "formerly the Portuguese sought to settle the land . . . but the natives of the country put an end to the attempt and killed all those who came there." [98]

In hopes of discovering the Northwest Passage and claiming it for England, in 1527 King Henry VIII sent out John Rut with two ships, the *Mary of Guildford* and the *Sampson.* Rut apparently did not enjoy the cold of the North, because after sailing no farther than 53° N, he reported to the king, "We durst go no further to the Northward for feare of more Ice."[99] So he headed south, along the coasts of Nova Scotia and New England, eventually turning up in the Caribbean. The Spanish were not happy to see a British ship there and scared Rut off with a well-placed cannonball.

France Enters the Picture

Despite the brief forays to the north by Fernandes and Fagundes, the Portuguese, like the Spanish, were primarily occupied in exploring and conquering lands to the south. That left the other two great powers of Europe, England and France, to divide up the northern continent. By the time del Cano returned from the first circumnavigation in 1522, the Spanish and the Portuguese had mapped the coast from the Strait of Magellan to Florida without finding a shortcut to China and India. Meanwhile, the area between Labrador and Newfoundland had been fairly thoroughly explored; at least it was certain there was no water route to the East—the long-sought Northwest Passage. At the time, of course, people had no way of knowing whether such a passage did or did not exist. One guess was as good as another. Thus King Francis I was hopeful that France could find a shorter way to China, thus making that country's trade in silks and spices more profitable.

In 1523 Francis commissioned an Italian nobleman named Giovanni da Verrazano to find that passage to China. Verrazano left with two ships in the fall of that year. As he said in a letter he wrote to Francis I on his return, he had had a very clear plan for the expedition:

> My intention on this voyage was to reach Cataia [Cathay, or China] and the extreme eastern coast of Asia, not expecting to find such a barrier of new land as I did find; and, if I did find such a land, I estimated that it would not lack a strait to penetrate to the Eastern Ocean [the Pacific].[100]

Verrazano landed at what is now Cape Fear, North Carolina, and made his way north. He stopped at several places along the way and made thorough descriptions of the people and the places he saw. He missed the Chesapeake Bay, but he sailed into New York Harbor and anchored at the place now known as Verrazano Narrows in 1524. From New York, he sailed eastward

Giovanni da Verrazano was commissioned by France to find the long-sought Northwest Passage to China. Instead, his journey took him to the shores of North America, where he explored much of the eastern coastline.

and surveyed Narragansett Bay, Block Island, Cape Cod, and the New England coast as far as present-day Maine.

Despite all his valuable and accurate reports, Verrazano made a significant mistake. He assumed that the water on the other side of the Outer Banks—the long, narrow islands off the North Carolina coast—was the Pacific Ocean. Since the North American mainland cannot be seen from a ship sailing eastward of the Outer Banks, it is understandable that Verrazano mistook the land he observed for an isthmus.

The Italian captain's error was reproduced on maps for nearly a hundred years, well into the seventeenth century. The Outer Banks are broken in several places by navigable inlets, but Verrazano apparently failed to explore any of them. Estevan Gomez, however, sailing for the Spanish Crown in the same year as Verrazano, explored the coast from Nova Scotia to the Caribbean and convinced the Spanish that Verrazano was mistaken about the ocean.

Although Verrazano did not discover a strait to the ocean, he did explore a great deal of coastline on France's behalf. When he returned to France, he hoped that he would be allowed to go back for further exploration, but Francis I was engaged in war with the Holy Roman Emperor, Charles V, and felt he could not spare any men or ships. This preoccupation on the part of France allowed the British to become the first to establish permanent colonies in these newly explored lands.

The Spanish Explore Inland

Estevan Gomez wrote enthusiastically about the lands that are now part of the United States. He noted that they were similar in climate to Europe. Similarities did not impress the people at home, however. "What need have we of what is found everywhere in Europe?"[101] wrote the sixteenth-century historian Peter Martyr. The Spanish in particular were far more interested in things that were not found in Europe: gold, for example, or such mystical and mythical things as the Fountain of Youth.

From their earliest days in the West Indies, the Spanish had heard that somewhere to the north there existed a spring

An early map illustrates the place, now known as Verrazano Narrows, where Verrazano anchored after sailing into New York Harbor.

Natives of North America

Giovanni da Verrazano describes the manners and customs of the people he saw when he landed on the coast of what is now North Carolina. This description comes from Verrazano's 1524 letter to King Francis I of France, translated by Susan Tarrow in The Voyages of Giovanni da Verrazzano, *by Lawrence C. Wroth.*

"They go completely naked except that around their loins they wear skins of small animals like martens, with a narrow belt of grass around the body, to which they tie various tails of other animals which hang down to the knees; the rest of the body is bare, and so is the head. Some of them wear garlands of birds' feathers. They are dark in color, not unlike the Ethiopians, with thick black hair, not very long, tied back behind the head like a small tail. As for the physique of these men, they are well proportioned, of medium height, a little taller than we are. They have broad chests, strong arms, and the legs and other parts of the body are well composed. There is nothing else, except that they tend to be rather broad in the face; but not all, for we saw many with angular faces. They have big black eyes, and an attentive and open look."

that would make even the oldest person young again. In 1513 Ponce de León, another of the Spanish seamen who had sailed with Columbus on the second voyage, set out from Cuba to search for the so-called Fountain of Youth. He did not find it, but in the effort he did map most of the coast of Florida. He never realized, however, that Florida was part of the mainland; he assumed it was another large island, like Cuba.

In 1519 Alonso de Pineda mapped most of the rest of the Gulf Coast. He was, like so many others, looking for a route to the Pacific. He entered the mouth of the Mississippi and visited native villages, where he heard rumors of gold to the north. Another Spaniard, Alvar Núñez Cabeza de Vaca, was stranded with a small band of settlers near Galveston and survived by living with the Indians. When he finally met up with a Spanish party in northern Mexico, he regaled them with tales he had heard during his sojourn of the Seven Cities of Cíbola—the golden cities that lay somewhere to the north.

When Cabeza de Vaca returned to Spain, he told his story to a soldier who already had some experience of the New World: Hernán de Soto. De Soto had served with Pedrárias in Darien and with Pizarro in Peru and was ambitious for his own wealth and power. As Cortés had done in Mexico, de Soto got royal authorization for his plans in the form of a commission. Then, having been declared governor of Florida, he set off with a large band of soldiers. On May 30, 1539, de Soto, leading six hundred men, "set out on a relentless, courageous, profitless march, which was to last four years and to take his men over 350,000 square miles of unexplored North America."[102] Unexplored by Europeans, that is: the expedition met many Indian tribes on the way and saw abandoned villages of even more. In some cases European diseases had preceded the Europeans. By the time they reached the villages of the Mississippi Valley, large numbers of native Americans had died of smallpox.

De Soto crossed Georgia and the Blue Ridge Mountains, reaching the banks of the Mississippi River at a spot just south of present-day Memphis in the spring of 1541. According to historian Penrose, "The Spaniards appear to have betrayed no awe whatever at the size of the river; to them it was merely an awkward military obstacle, which put them to a month's hard work making barges for its crossing."[103] They went on into the heart of the continent, spending the winter of 1541–1542 in what is now eastern Oklahoma, without ever seeming to get any closer to the Seven Cities of Cíbola. They turned around at that point, but on the return journey de Soto died. The remaining members of the band attempted to reach Mexico overland

Verrazano Takes a Captive

The French, like the Spanish, thought nothing of taking New World residents back to Europe, as slaves or just as proof that they had been to foreign shores. Here, Verrazano tells of the capture of a child in the land he called Arcadia, which was probably near Kitty Hawk, North Carolina. The account is from Verrazano's 1524 letter to King Francis I, translated by Susan Tarrow in Lawrence C. Wroth's The Voyages of Giovanni Verrazzano.

"We anchored there, and with 20 men we penetrated about two leagues inland, to find that the people had fled in terror to the forests. Searching everywhere, we met with a very old woman and a young girl of 18 or 20 years, who had hidden in the grass in fear. The old woman had two little girls whom she carried on her shoulders, and clinging to her neck a boy—they were all about 8 years old. The young woman also had three children, but all girls. When we met them, they began to shout. The old woman made signs to us that the men had fled to the woods. We gave her some of our food to eat, which she accepted with great pleasure; the young woman refused everything and threw [it] angrily on the ground. We took the boy from the old woman to carry back to France, and we wanted to take the young woman, who was very beautiful and tall, but it was impossible to take her to the sea because of the loud cries she uttered. And as we were a long way from the ship and had to pass through several woods, we decided to leave her behind, and took only the boy."

Hernán de Soto led a large expedition over 350,000 square miles of land in North America in search of the fabled seven golden cities of the north. Here, de Soto and his men reach the banks of the Mississippi River.

and spent another year wandering around in what is now Texas before finally returning to the Mississippi and floating downriver on barges, following the Gulf Coast to Mexico. Three hundred of the original six hundred survived this grueling march, which taught the Spanish a great deal about the continent. Still, since they had discovered no gold, they regarded the whole thing as a dismal failure.

At the same time that de Soto was journeying west from the East Coast, other expeditions were looking for the Seven Cities by traveling overland from Mexico. The most notable of these expeditions was the one led by Francisco Vásquez de Coronado. In 1540–1541 Coronado traveled over previously established routes as far as eastern Arizona. There he sent several parties out in different directions in hopes that one of them would find the Seven Cities. One of the parties, led by García López de Cárdenas, did not find gold, but instead

the dramatic sight of the Grand Canyon. Coronado himself led a party through what are now Texas and Oklahoma, and went as far as eastern Kansas.

Like de Soto's before him, Coronado's journey was deemed a failure because it did not produce any gold. What it did produce, however, was a vastly important contribution to the knowledge of Europe. Between them, de Soto and Coronado mapped a large portion of the North American continent and brought back knowledge of natural wonders such as the Grand Canyon.

The French in Canada

Although Francis I of France had been too busy with war to send Verrazano back to America, the French were ready to start exploring again by 1534. They were still

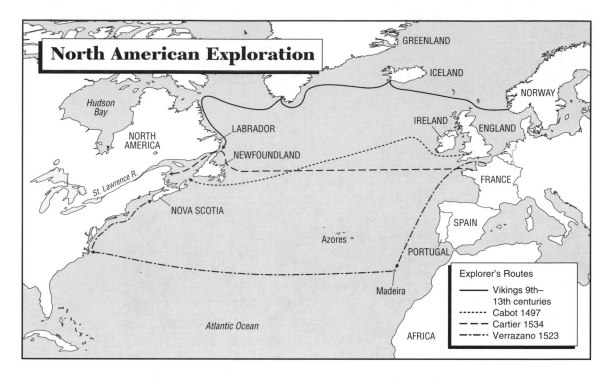

North American Exploration

Hudson Bay

NORTH AMERICA

GREENLAND

ICELAND

NORWAY

LABRADOR

IRELAND

ENGLAND

NEWFOUNDLAND

St. Lawrence R.

FRANCE

NOVA SCOTIA

SPAIN

Azores

PORTUGAL

Madeira

Atlantic Ocean

AFRICA

Explorer's Routes

——— Vikings 9th–13th centuries

·········· Cabot 1497

– – – Cartier 1534

–·–·– Verrazano 1523

looking for the Northwest Passage, and to this end Jacques Cartier left France in 1534 bound for the island of Newfoundland. He sailed past it, proceeding into the Gulf of Saint Lawrence as far as Prince Edward Island, which the crew found to be a delightful place. They sailed north next, turning west into Chaleur Bay, thinking it was the passage they sought. When they discovered it was only a bay, dividing the Gaspé Peninsula from what is now the Canadian province of New Brunswick, they headed back to France.

The following year, Cartier went back to North America, taking with him as guides several Indians his crew had captured on the first voyage. These Indians told of three large kingdoms, and from their descriptions, the French believed they would find something similar to the Aztec and Inca Empires of the southern continent. On this occasion, Cartier sailed into the Saint Lawrence River, going as far as the future site of Montreal. He realized by this time, of course, that the Saint Lawrence was a river, not a strait, and he was further discouraged by the view from the top of Mount Royal: "The continental land mass stretched away as far as the eye could see."[104] He spent the winter there but hurried back to France in mid-1536, as soon as the ice melted enough to let him sail.

Cartier hoped that Francis would sponsor a colony in America, but once again war with Charles V delayed any action. In 1541, however, Cartier headed back to Canada with colonizers. A French nobleman, the Sieur de Roberval, was to follow Cartier and serve as military commander of the new colony. Cartier set up a colony at Cap Rouge but did not give the project much attention, preferring instead to explore the area and look for gold. He went back to France in the spring, taking "gold"

The Good and Perfect Navigator

Historian Samuel Eliot Morison, in his book The European Discovery of America: The Northern Voyages, *uses Samuel Champlain's description of the "good and perfect navigator" to describe Jacques Cartier.*

"He had better not be a delicate eater or drinker, otherwise he will be frequently upset by changes of climate and food. . . . Be continually on his guard against scurvy, and be provided with remedies against it. He should be robust and alert, have good sea-legs and be indefatigable [tireless] . . . so that whatever accident may befall he can keep the deck and in a strong voice order everyone to do his duty. He must not be above lending a hand to the work himself, to make the seamen more prompt in their attention. . . .

He should be pleasant and affable in conversation, absolute in his commands, not too ready to talk with shipmates, except the officers; otherwise he might be despised. He should punish ill-doers severely, and reward good men, gratifying them from time to time with a pat on the back, praising them but not overdoing it, so as to give no occasion for envy. . . . He should never let himself be overcome by wine, for if an officer or seaman becomes a drunkard it is dangerous to entrust him with responsibility; he might be sleeping like a pig when an accident occurs. . . . He should turn night into day, watch the greater part of the night, always sleep clothed so as to be ready to come on deck promptly if anything happens."

An able navigator, Jacques Cartier (pictured) was sent by France in search of the hoped-for Northwest Passage that Verrazano and others had been unable to find.

A painting portrays Cartier and his crew sailing into the beautiful Saint Lawrence River, which Cartier at first hoped was a strait that might be the Northwest Passage that he was looking for.

(iron pyrite) and "diamonds" (quartz crystals). Roberval arrived at Cap Rouge and wintered there with the colonists, who were by now getting discouraged by the hostilities of the Huron Indians. The Hurons had been welcoming when the Europeans first arrived but got considerably less friendly when they learned that the foreigners meant to stay. Roberval and the remaining colonists abandoned Cap Rouge and sailed back to France in the fall of 1543.

Because of problems at home, the French were late taking part in exploring the newfound continents. In the seventeenth and eighteenth centuries, however, the French would make a place for themselves exploring the inland areas of the North American continent. French explorers mapped much of Canada and explored the entire Mississippi River, from its origins in the north to its mouth at New Orleans. The French influence can still be felt there.

Chapter

7 Later Explorations

Once Cortés had conquered the Aztecs and established settlements in Mexico, he set up shipyards and started building boats on the Pacific side, so that he and others could explore the coast. He was still hoping to find precious metals, and he did not want anyone else to get to them first. Cortés received permission to explore the Pacific coast northward and to keep 10 percent of any gold or other valuable goods he might find there. He was occupied during the late 1520s and early 1530s in various other pursuits. In 1535, however, he took two ships north and sighted the long peninsula known as Baja [Lower] California and took possession for Charles V. He found no gold or other valuables there, however, and political matters called him back to Mexico City and then to Spain.

California

Second in command in Mexico was an officer named Francisco de Ulloa. In the summer of 1539, Ulloa took three ships and explored the Gulf of California, which separates Baja from the mainland. Ulloa was not impressed with the Gulf of California, describing the shore as "very poor . . . mountains or bare rock, without trees or

green except *cardon* (the giant cactus)."[105] Ulloa probably never made it as far north as the present state of California, but he undoubtedly saw something of its mountains when he rowed a little way up the mouth of the Colorado River. According to historian Samuel Eliot Morison, "He was less impressed by them [the mountains] than by a multitude of sea-lions (100,000 at least!) at the river mouth."[106] In any case, he did not make any attempt to explore inland.

The real exploration of the California coast came in 1542, when the viceroy of Mexico appointed Juan Rodríguez Cabrillo to lead an expedition north up the coast. Cabrillo was a soldier who had come to Mexico in 1520 and had joined Cortés in the march to Tenochtitlán. Morison says, "The object of the expedition seems to have been exploration pure and simple, including, of course, the hope of discovering new sources of gold and silver, or a seaport in . . . the fabled country of the Seven Cities."[107]

Cabrillo left Mexico with two ships on June 27, 1542, and explored the western Baja coast. On September 27, he sailed into a "closed and very good harbor," which he named San Miguel. Today it is known as San Diego. They had a stormy voyage along the coast, but they sighted the Santa Barbara Channel Islands, Point

Concepción, and Big Sur. There they encountered another heavy storm, and "so great was the swell of the ocean that it was terrifying to see and the coast was bold and the mountains very high."[108] Although some historians think that Cabrillo was the first European to see San Francisco Bay, it is likely that because of the fog, "like everyone else for two more centuries, Cabrillo missed the Golden Gate."[109]

Not too far north of San Francisco Bay, Cabrillo turned back and returned to the Channel Islands to spend the winter. He died there in January 1543, when a broken arm, improperly cleaned, became infected. Bartolomé Ferrelo, whom the dying Cabrillo had appointed as next commander, went north again in January or February, possibly getting as far as Klamath, Califor-

nia, near the Oregon border. Ferrelo and Cabrillo contributed greatly to Spain's knowledge of the American coastline. They did not, however, contribute to the coffers of Spain, having found no silver or gold, so their travels were forgotten and Spain made no further attempts to explore that coast for another fifty years.

Cabot Explores the Rio de la Plata

Much more profitable to the Spanish was the exploration of the valley of the Rio de la Plata (River Plate) in Brazil. The Rio de la Plata is actually an estuary, formed where several great rivers, notably the

Landing at San Diego

In 1542 Juan Rodríguez Cabrillo took two ships north from Mexico to explore the coast. The journal of that voyage has been lost, but this description comes from a summary of the journal written afterward in the third person, probably by Bartolomé Ferrelo. This translation is from West of the West: Witnesses to the California Experience, *by Robert Kirsch and William S. Murphy.*

"On Thursday they sailed about six leagues along a north-north-west coast and discovered a very good closed port . . . which they named San Miguel [later San Diego]. After anchoring they went ashore where there were some people, three of whom awaited them, while the rest fled. To these some presents were given, and they explained by signs that inland people like the Spaniards [Coronado's men] had passed. . . . [They] explained by signs that some people like us, that is, bearded, dressed and armed like those aboard the vessels, were going about inland. They showed by signs that these carried cross-bows, and swords; they made gestures with the right arm as if using lances, and went running about as if they were going on horseback."

Juan Rodríguez Cabrillo's expedition (pictured) provided detailed knowledge of the California coastline, but because they found no gold or silver, the new territory was of limited interest to Spain.

Paraná and the Uruguay, empty into the sea at what is today Buenos Aires. The Spanish first encountered this estuary in 1515, when Juan Díaz de Solís was searching along the South American coast for a passage to the Pacific. The natives killed de Solís there when he went ashore, and his crew sailed back to Spain. Four years later, Magellan spent some time there on the first leg of his journey of circumnavigation, also hoping that it would cut through the continent and shorten his trip.

It was not until 1526, however, that the area was thoroughly explored, by none other than Sebastian Cabot. He had apparently decided that the future in exploration lay with the Holy Roman Empire,

not England, and had signed on to the service of Charles V. According to historian Boies Penrose,

> With a view of determining the Line of Demarcation and of laying claim to the Spice Islands, he [Cabot] was dispatched in 1526 with the very extravagant commission "to discover the Moluccas, Tarsis, Ophir, Cipango, and Cathay, to barter and load his ships with gold, silver, precious stones, pearls, drugs, spices, silks, brocades, and other precious things."[110]

The emperor was still hoping to find a route not only to China (Cathay), Japan (Cipango), and the Spice Islands (the Moluccas),

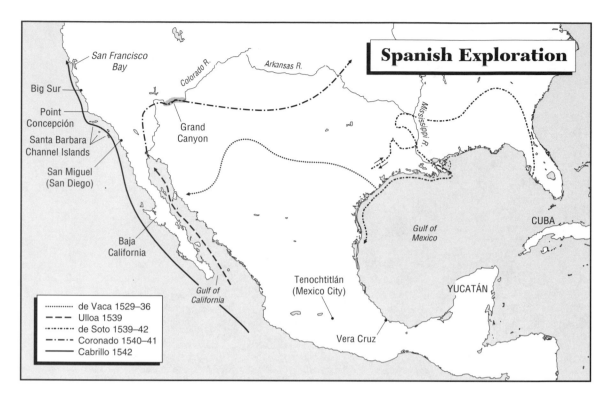

Spanish Exploration

San Francisco Bay
Big Sur
Point Concepción
Santa Barbara Channel Islands
San Miguel (San Diego)
Colorado R.
Arkansas R.
Mississippi R.
Grand Canyon
Baja California
Gulf of California
Tenochtitlán (Mexico City)
Gulf of Mexico
CUBA
YUCATÁN
Vera Cruz

.... de Vaca 1529–36
- - - Ulloa 1539
-·-·-·- de Soto 1539–42
-··-··- Coronado 1540–41
——— Cabrillo 1542

but also of Tarshish and Ophir, mentioned in the Bible as the source of King Solomon's fortune but unknown in modern times.

The expedition made it to the coast of Brazil despite heavy winds and worked its way north and west along the coast, stopping at several harbors along the way. On the Uruguay coast, Cabot met some members of the de Solis expedition who had been stranded there for ten years. They told Cabot stories of gold and silver in the interior regions. A survivor who had become friendly with the local Indians and had learned their language reported to Cabot that somewhere up the river "was a mountain of silver, ruled over by a monarch so covered and bedecked with [silver] plate as to be called *El Rey Blanco* [the White King]."[111] This White King was probably the Inca, and there certainly was silver in the mountains, as

Pizarro's men would discover when they came from the west only a few years later.

At this point, Cabot was probably still planning to continue his voyage to all the various points east, but in attempting to move into a more sheltered harbor, his flagship struck a rock and sank. Morison says, "And this, for Cabot, clinched the argument to concentrate on silver hunting in the River Plate. He could hardly be expected to cross the Pacific without his largest and best ship."[112]

His first move was to explore the Paraná River, which empties into the Rio de la Plata just above Buenos Aires. He took two ships up the river as far as its convergence with the Carcaraña River, where he built a fort that he called Sancti Spiritus. Then Cabot took a small oared boat called a bergantina and continued to work his way up the Paraná. As he stopped along the way, he met Guaraní Indians, who gave him objects made of silver. Historian Penrose says, "When asked where it [the silver] came from, the Indians pointed westward and talked of the 'White King'; the silver was in fact Peruvian, and was therefore the first lot of Inca treasure to reach Europe."[113]

Cabot made it almost a thousand miles upstream, to a point in present-day Paraguay, before swift currents and hostile Indians forced him to turn back. When he did, however, he found that he had a rival on the river. Diego García had arrived from Seville with the intention to explore inland from the Rio de la Plata. He was none too pleased to find that Cabot had done it before him, especially since Cabot was supposed to have been on his way to the Moluccas. According to Morison,

Sebastian Cabot's journeys in South America proved to Spain that there was silver and possibly other riches to be found there, leading them to set up a colony in Buenos Aires.

The two exchanged coldly polite notes: García to Cabot: "Your honor should leave this river, for mine is the conquest." Cabot to García: "Your grace should not go further up the river, for I discovered it, and it is a year and a half since I took possession. . . . I require you to get out of this river." They finally agreed to cooperate, and actually made a joint voyage up the Paraná; but it is a matter of conjecture how far north they sailed. As long as both men were within La Plata, the situation was tense, and García, when he reached home, accused Cabot of having stripped the sails from his vessel, and of committing other high crimes and misdemeanors.[114]

Whatever personal difficulties he might have had, Cabot's explorations alerted his sponsors in Spain to the possibilities of the continent. That silver was to be found was certain. The Plata Valley was a likely spot to set up a colony, and the Spanish tried at once to do so. The first colony, which founded Buenos Aires in 1535, was unsuccessful. The colonists had difficulty in finding water and food, and the Indians were unfriendly. In 1537 Juan de Ayolas took most of the colonists and moved upriver. There he made a treaty of friendship with the Guaraní Indians and founded the town of Asunción on the Paraguay River. From Asunción, Ayolas founded a second colony at Buenos Aires, and this time it was successful. Meanwhile, the Spanish had appointed a new governor for the region, Alvar Nuñez Cabeza de Vaca, the man who had earlier brought back stories of the Seven Cities of Gold. Having spent eight years journeying from Florida to Mexico, Cabeza de Vaca was used to making his way through wilderness. He chose an overland route from Brazil to Asunción that was developed and used by the Spanish in later years.

The Search for the Southern Continent

Before the sixteenth century, the people of Europe had assumed that the earth was composed mainly of land. Their excursions in the early years of that century, and especially Magellan's circumnavigation, had begun to reveal to them the extent of the world's oceans. Nevertheless, the myth persisted that there must be a large continent in the Southern Hemisphere, to balance the landmasses in the Northern Hemisphere. This large continent was even put on some maps, labeled Terra Australis Incognita (the unknown southern land). It was supposed to be somewhere in the South Pacific, and each successive voyage that failed to discover the great continent pushed its imagined boundaries farther away.

Portuguese seafarers might have gone looking for the southern continent, but they were too busy in Brazil, India, and the Moluccas. Spanish explorers were occupied in Peru and Mexico, and were beginning to develop trade with the Philippines. Since they were already in the Pacific, they might have explored farther south, but "the southeast trade winds lifted ships steadily northward toward the equator and made it almost impossible for vessels leaving from Mexico to enter the southern ocean."[115] As a result, it was the British who first determined to go in search of the southern continent.

Queen Elizabeth of England, a daughter of Henry VIII, chose for this venture a mariner named Francis Drake. Drake had made a name for himself as something of a pirate, raiding Spanish ships and settlements in the Caribbean and bringing silver back to the queen. Since England was constantly on the verge of war with Spain, the queen was quite pleased with Drake's activities, and he was a favorite of hers. Drake was popular with the men who sailed for him, as well. His daring, his skill, and his personal charm all contributed to the luster of the man who, according to historian Boies Penrose, "stands forth as one of the greatest seamen of all time."[116]

So in 1577 the queen sent Drake on what turned out to be the second circumnavigation of the world. The original plan called for Drake to sail through the Strait of Magellan, then find and follow the coast of Terra Australis and return home the way he had come. Before he left England, however, Drake had a new secret set of plans. It is unclear whether the original idea came from Drake, Queen Elizabeth, or the secretary of state, Francis Walsingham, but apparently the three of them agreed that Drake would not look for the southern continent after all. He would head north after passing through the Strait of Magellan and "carry the undeclared war against Spain into the Pacific"[117] by raiding Spanish ships and settlements along the coast of South America.

Drake's Voyage

Drake left England in the fall of 1577 with five vessels, including his flagship, the *Pelican*, which he would later rename the

A Man of Action

Historian Boies Penrose, in his book Travel and Discovery in the Renaissance, *describes Sir Francis Drake and gives the modern reader some idea of why Drake was so loved and admired in his own time (by the English if not by the Spanish).*

"His education was at best sketchy: he learned to read and write, but precious little more. However, he was not cast in the reflective or studious mold. Rather was he a man of action, and in addition to his qualities of leadership, he possessed one gift to the ultimate degree—he could probably sail a boat better than any other man who has ever lived. When this is added to his characteristics of commanding men, of lightning opportunism rising at times to inspiration, of cheerfulness in misfortune and kindly charity in success, it is easy to see why he stands forth as one of the greatest seamen of all time."

Sir Francis Drake, who led the second circumnavigation of the world, won many admirers, including the queen of England, with his charm, bravery, and skillful seamanship.

Golden Hind. His voyage has some interesting parallels to Magellan's voyage. Like Magellan, Drake stopped at Port San Julian on the coast of Patagonia, and like Magellan's crew, Drake's crew mutinied there. Like Magellan, Drake put down the mutiny and continued the journey through the strait. In the strait, Drake lost one of his ships to weather and another sailed back to England, just as one of Magellan's had done. At this point, Drake was left with only his flagship, as the other two ships, a storeship and a small pinnace, had been abandoned as unnecessary or unseaworthy.

So he proceeded north along the west coast of South America, raiding Spanish settlements and ships as he went:

Drake's tactics were to surprise, capture, and sack a Spanish settlement with all shipping in the harbor, and when he had looted everything valuable, turn ships and sailors loose, but with no sails to enable them to pursue him.[118]

These tactics worked because the settlements were lightly armed and guarded. Until now, the Spanish had had to worry about attack only from the Indians, and their superior weapons were more than enough to meet that threat. Drake's arrival was an enormous surprise, and the Spanish were caught completely off guard.

Having "earned" in this way more than enough to pay for the cost of his voyage, Drake continued north, the first European to explore the coast of North America in forty years. He went as far north as

Drake's flagship, the Golden Hind, *takes to the high seas to carry out Drake's mission of waging England's undeclared war against Spain in the Pacific by raiding Spanish ships and settlements along the coast of South America.*

The English Pirate

One of Francis Drake's crew members describes the ease with which the English were able to raid the Spanish along the coast of Peru in the summer of 1578. A portion of this extraordinary passage—taken from The Sea-Dragon: Journals of Francis Drake's Voyage Around the World, *by George Sanderlin—is translated into modern English below.*

"January 19: As we sailed along, continually searching for fresh water, we came to a place called Tarapaca, and landing there we lighted upon a Spaniard who lay asleep, and had lying by him 13 bars of silver, weighing in all about 4000 Spanish ducats. We would not (could we have chosen) have awaked him of his nap. But seeing we, against our wills, did him that injury, we freed him of his charge [the silver], which otherwise perhaps would have kept him waking, and so left him to take . . . the other part of his sleep in more security."

. . . We would have preferred not to awaken the Spaniard, but we had no choice. However, since we had been forced to interrupt his nap, we compensated for our rudeness by taking the silver, which was not his to begin with. Besides, if we had allowed him to keep it, he might have stayed awake worrying about being robbed. With that, we left him to return to his nap, with better peace of mind.

Vancouver Island, probably searching for the western end of the hoped-for Northwest Passage, before cold and fog drove him back south. He spent June and July 1579 in a bay on the coast of California, overhauling the *Golden Hind* and preparing for the long trip across the Pacific. There has been much debate over the years about where Drake actually spent this time, but it is now fairly widely accepted that it was the bay now known as Drake's Bay, in northern California. Drake, like others before and after him, undoubtedly missed the entrance to San Francisco Bay in the fog. He named the land Nova Albion and claimed it for England. He and his men had friendly relations with the Miwok Indians of the region, who reportedly "took a sorrowful farewell of us . . . [and] ran to the top of the hills to keep us in their sight as long as they could."[119]

The *Golden Hind* had an uneventful trip across the Pacific to the Moluccas, where Drake took on a cargo of cloves. He rounded Africa's Cape of Good Hope in June 1580 and sailed into Plymouth Harbor in England on September 26. Drake was already a hero in England, and this voyage only enhanced his reputation. The

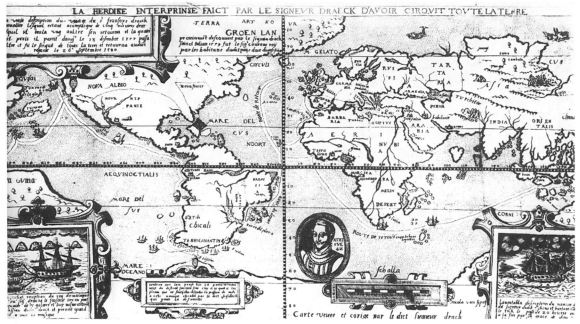

This map, which depicts Drake's circumnavigation of the world, is largely accurate thanks to the huge advances in geography made possible by the great age of exploration.

"circumnavigation fired the imagination of Englishmen as no other naval exploit had so far done."[120] But England was still involved in hostilities with Spain, and the queen turned her attention from exploration to warfare.

The southern continent remained out of reach for another two hundred years. In 1642 Abel Tasman, of the Dutch East India Company, found Tasmania and New Zealand, and in the 1770s the Englishman James Cook mapped much of the coast of Australia. There was indeed a continent there, but of much smaller size than the legends had predicted.

By the time Drake completed his circumnavigation in 1580, the map of the world had a vastly different look from the maps of a century earlier. A map made in 1580 is immediately recognizable to modern eyes. Australia will be missing, California may still be depicted as an island, and the northern reaches of the West Coast of North America will be sketchy, but the familiar outlines of Africa, South America, and most of North America will be there, along with those of Europe and Asia. Also at this time, in European mapmaking, the center of the world map shifts from the Mediterranean to the Atlantic.

A New World

In 1580—less than a century after Columbus's first voyage and only 150 years after Prince Henry the Navigator began to send explorers out along the frightening coast of Africa—the world was truly a new and different place. Foods, diseases, plants, animals, medicines, and technologies crossed the Atlantic in both directions, changing the lives of both Europeans and Americans and having an influence on the whole world. That it was Europeans and not Asians or Americans who expanded the world map had far-reaching implications. The languages, the religion, and many of the customs of Europe found fertile ground in the Americas, and a strong bond was forged between the two continents. Five hundred years later, people all over the world are still living daily with the consequences of the great age of exploration.

Why Europe?

Why was it Europeans who explored and mapped the world, and not Chinese or Japanese or Arab sailors? Why didn't Aztec, Inca, or Mayan seamen appear on the coasts of Portugal or Africa, bringing their religions and customs to another continent? The answers have to do with technology, global patterns of wind and weather, and customs and values.

By the fifteenth century, the Arabs were well established throughout the entire Mediterranean world, as well as India. Their ships were coasting vessels, for they never needed to go out onto the open ocean. They did not need to sail around Africa to get to Portugal: they were just across the Strait of Gibraltar in North Africa—and they controlled most of the Mediterranean. They had trade with India and with most of Asia, and access to the spices and minerals that Europeans sought. They were, in a sense, "already there."[121] In addition, their vessels were unsuited to travel on the high seas. The boats of the Arabs were held together with cords rather than with nails and would not withstand the rigors of ocean travel. And although the Arabs certainly had access, through their possessions, to other resources, their own lands held only limited amounts of the raw materials, milled goods, and natural features essential to shipbuilding and to long voyages: wood, resin, iron, textiles, fresh water, and good harbors.

The Chinese were great seafarers in the fourteenth century. Before Henry the Navigator sent ships out along the west coast of

Africa, the Chinese had already explored the Indian Ocean and the east coast of Africa. Between 1405 and 1433, Emperor Yung-lo sent out thousands of men in hundreds of ships, under the command of Cheng Ho. But whereas the Portuguese voyages were motivated by the need to further trade and exploration, the voyages of Cheng Ho's navy "became an institution in themselves, designed to display the splendor and power of the new Ming dynasty." By the middle of the fourteenth century, however, the Chinese had begun what is known as the Great Withdrawal. It became illegal for Chinese to travel outside the country. Convinced by their earlier explorations that there was no civilization as great and sophisticated as their own, the Chinese believed that the rest of the world had nothing to offer to them. And so, in the words of historian Daniel Boorstin, "fully equipped with the technology, the intelligence, and the national resources to become discoverers, the Chinese doomed themselves to be the discovered."[122]

Japan was undergoing enormous political upheaval in the fourteenth and fifteenth centuries. The Japanese were in no position to look beyond their own borders. By the time order was restored in the sixteenth century, the Japanese made the decision to turn inward, as China had done, to avoid contamination from the rest of the world.

The civilizations of the Americas, while often advanced in architecture and astronomy, were not seagoing peoples. Their only vessels were rafts with which they could sail with the wind and drift with the currents. They did not use metals—copper, bronze, and iron—for tools. Their tools were made of stone and wood. More importantly, they did not have extensive written languages. In Europe, writing was important not only in administration and trade, but also in "motivating and guiding exploration and conquest, and making available a range of information and human experience extending into remote places and times."[123]

Although the Chinese were great seafarers in the fourteenth century, they became convinced that the rest of the world's civilizations were not as great and sophisticated as their own, and concluded that they would gain little from further exploration.

Though relatively advanced, American civilizations like the Aztecs were not seagoing and did not have extensive written languages, both of which prevented them from exploring the outside world.

Disease

Cortés and Pizarro were aided in their conquests of Mexico and Peru by germs. Smallpox in particular killed more Aztecs and Incas than the armed forces of either Spanish conquistador. Similarly, de Soto found abandoned villages in the Mississippi River Valley, all the inhabitants having died in epidemics transmitted by coastal Indians who had been infected by Spaniards visiting the coast. "The Spaniards' microbes spread to the interior in advance of the Spaniards themselves."[124]

No one knows for sure how many people lived in North and South America before 1492. Estimates vary, but current estimates suggest that North America was home to around 20 million before Europeans arrived. By 1600 there were only about 1.4 million left. The four greatest killers of the sixteenth century were smallpox, measles, influenza, and bubonic plague. All of these diseases were common in Europe and Asia, but previously unknown in the Western Hemisphere. When serious diseases become established in an isolated region, the residents develop immunities. Those who manage to survive the first outbreak acquire resistance, which they pass on to their children. After a few generations, most people in a population who get the disease will have a relatively mild, nonfatal form. The Indians had never been exposed to these diseases, and the first outbreaks, brought by the Spaniards, were devastating.

Why didn't these diseases exist in the Americas? Physiologist and author Jared Diamond believes it is because most epidemic diseases evolve from diseases of animals. When people domesticate animals, they live in close contact with them, and animal diseases mutate into human afflictions. Smallpox, measles, and the other major epidemic diseases were originally diseases of cattle and pigs. There were only five kinds of domesticated animals at that time in the Americas: "the turkey in Mexico and the U.S. Southwest, the llama/alpaca and the guinea pig in the Andes, the Muscovy duck in tropical South America, and the dog throughout the Americas."[125] Diamond points out that none of these were likely sources for human disease because they do not congregate in large flocks and generally do not live in close contact with humans. Moreover, there were never as many turkeys, llamas, and so on in the Americas as there were pigs and cattle and sheep in Eurasia.

The one disease that probably did travel across the Atlantic from the Americas to Europe and Asia is syphilis. Historians and scientists have debated for years about whether syphilis existed in Eurasia before 1492. It is difficult to know for certain, because many of its symptoms match those of other diseases. Syphilis leaves characteristic scars on the bones of the lower leg, however, and in recent years scientists have examined the bones of skeletons from all over the world, ranging in age from 400 to 6,000 years old. The skeletons from the Americas "all showed clear signs of syphilis, at least 800 and

perhaps 1,600 years ago,"[126] but the skeletons from Africa, Asia, Europe, and the Middle East showed no signs of the disease before the time of Columbus. Certainly there is a well-documented outbreak of the disease in Europe after Columbus's return.

Food

When the first explorers arrived in the New World, they hoped to bring back riches: gold, silver, precious jewels. What they brought back instead was even more valuable in the long run: new foods that changed the way Europeans ate. They repaid the favor by introducing new foods and crops to the Americas. The Mexican food we know today is dependent on the pork, chicken, beef, and cheese brought by the Spanish. What we think of as Italian food is dependent on the tomato, a native American food. Spicy Sichuan Chinese food would not be the same without chiles from South America. The "traditional" Irish potato came from America, as did the chocolate for which the Swiss became famous. Food historian Raymond Sokolov says, "The French, Italian and Spanish food 'traditions' we now think of as primeval all sprang up relatively recently and would be unrecognizable without the American foods sent across the water, mostly in Spanish boats."[127]

Besides food crops, other American plants came to have a major influence in the rest of the world, especially tobacco and cotton. Before the fifteenth century, clothing in Europe was made chiefly of wool or linen (from the flax plant). Asian countries had silk, but only the wealthiest

New Foods

Food traditions changed dramatically after the Spanish began bringing new animals and plant crops to the Americas. Food historian Raymond Sokolov, in his book Why We Eat What We Eat, *discusses some of those contributions.*

"In 1493, Columbus returned to the New World on his second voyage and brought with him horses, dogs, pigs, cattle, chickens, sheep, and goats. These pioneering animals were intended to supply Spaniards with familiar foods, but their real contribution was much more original and important. Their meat, milk, and cheese made Mexican food possible: cheese-filled quesadillas, barbecued beef carnitas, pork-stuffed tamales, chicken tacos. Columbus came with seventeen ships and twelve hundred men, and in the holds of those ships were, literally, the seeds of colonization. Columbus brought what was needed to start plantations, orchards, and kitchen gardens, the wherewithal to grow onions, grapes, fruit, radishes, and sugarcane."

of Europeans could afford it. Cotton was native to both Eurasia and the Americas, and Indian and Egyptian cotton was among the products the early explorers hoped to trade for. The presence of cotton in the Americas, however, allowed European settlers to raise cotton in sufficient quantities to clothe a civilization, although for many years the industry depended upon slave labor.

Tobacco was another cash crop developed by the use of slave labor. Columbus was the first European to report seeing native Americans smoking the leaf of the tobacco plant. In the sixteenth and seventeenth centuries, when Europeans began to colonize the Americas in earnest, tobacco became very popular in Europe and became a major export from the colonies.

In addition to crops, the Europeans brought domesticated animals with them.

The Europeans' encounters with the natives in the New World provided them with many valuable things that they took back to Europe, including new foods, cotton, and tobacco.

Sheep, pigs, and cattle came on some of the earliest Spanish boats and were immediately absorbed into the native cultures. Before that time, meat was rarely part of the normal diet, except for occasional game (mainly duck, turkey, and deer). In Peru the guinea pig was a specialty, and in Mexico meals of corn and beans were sometimes supplemented with insect eggs and larvae.

Horses and Other Animals

European animals—sheep, goats, and pigs—multiplied rapidly in the New World. There were few natural predators, and the animals had short breeding cycles. Cattle took longer, but the Spanish were breeding cattle in Mexico as early as 1521, and the vast grazing lands made it economically advantageous to raise large herds.

Horses transformed the native American way of life. Some North American Indians used dogs to pull small loads, and the Incas had domesticated llamas, which were also used for some hauling. But the Indians immediately recognized the value—for transportation and communication, hunting, fighting, and hauling—of the horses brought by Spanish officers. Although the Spanish at first tried to keep horses from the Indians, the animals soon became commonplace and some "Native American societies became renowned for their mastery of horses. . . . Those mounted plains warriors . . . now figure prominently in white Americans' image of American Indians, but the basis for that image was created only after 1492."[128]

The Inevitable Meeting

In 1492 Christopher Columbus waded ashore onto an island in the Caribbean and started a clash of cultures that is still being debated today. Some regard Columbus as a hero; others regard him as a villain. Certainly Columbus deserves credit for his unwavering belief in the value of his Enterprise of the Indies, his bravery in facing the unknown, and his seamanship. But it is clear that if Columbus had not "discovered" the Americas, another European would have done so within a few months or years. The Portuguese were busy exploring the coast of Africa, and it was only eight years later, in 1500, that Pedro Cabral sighted Brazil as he sailed southeast and rounded the bulge of West Africa. The Spanish, Portuguese, and British were all in the process of becoming seafaring nations, and none would have been content to stay in sight of the known coasts for long.

Americans and Europeans first met on a large scale and on a lasting basis in the late fifteenth and early sixteenth centuries, with results the world has been living with ever since. Who can say what might have happened if the meeting had occurred when one or the other culture was more or less advanced? Who can say whether the meeting might have been different if there had been women on board the European ships?

The voyages of exploration at the turn of the sixteenth century paved the way for the world as we know it today. Some of the results of this age of exploration were negative: wars, conquests, slavery, and brutality. Others were positive: the meeting and

Although Columbus (pictured) and other explorers are often villified for the negative consequences of their voyages, such as war and brutality, they should be recognized for helping to bring the world closer together.

blending of cultures, the spread of languages, and the introduction of all parts of the world to all other parts. But for good or for bad, a few men had the curiosity and the energy to push beyond the borders of the world they knew, and as a result they brought the whole world closer together.

Notes

Chapter 1: Terra Incognita: The Unknown World

1. Daniel J. Boorstin, *The Discoverers*. New York: Vintage Books, 1985, p. 94.

2. Boies Penrose, *Travel and Discovery in the Renaissance, 1420–1620*. New York: Atheneum, 1962, p. 6.

3. Penrose, *Travel and Discovery in the Renaissance*, p. 15.

4. Penrose, *Travel and Discovery in the Renaissance*, p. 17.

5. J. H. Parry, *The Age of Reconnaissance*. Berkeley: University of California Press, 1963, 1981, p. 8.

6. John Mandeville, *The Travels of Sir John Mandeville*. New York: Dover Publications, 1964, p. 5.

7. John R. Hale and the editors of Time-Life Books, *The Age of Exploration*. New York: Time, Inc., 1966, p. 14.

8. Hale, *The Age of Exploration*, p. 14.

9. Penrose, *Travel and Discovery in the Renaissance*, p. 43.

10. Boorstin, *The Discoverers*, p. 166.

11. Penrose, *Travel and Discovery in the Renaissance*, p. 48.

12. Quoted in Boorstin, *The Discoverers*, p. 167.

13. Quoted in Boorstin, *The Discoverers*, p. 167.

14. Hale, *The Age of Exploration*, p. 35.

15. Parry, *The Age of Reconnaissance*, p. 132.

Chapter 2: The Enterprise of the Indies: Christopher Columbus

16. Quoted in Christopher Columbus, *The Voyage of Christopher Columbus: Columbus's Own Journal of Discovery*. Newly restored and translated by John Cummins. New York: St. Martin's Press, 1992, p. 23.

17. Quoted in *Columbus, The Voyage of Christopher Columbus*, p. 26.

18. Quoted in *Columbus, The Voyage of Christopher Columbus*, p. 31.

19. Samuel Eliot Morison, *The European Discovery of America: The Southern Voyages, A.D. 1492–1616*. New York: Oxford University Press, 1974, p. 31.

20. Morison, *The Southern Voyages*, p. 35.

21. Quoted in Morison, *The Southern Voyages*, p. 40.

22. Morison, *The Southern Voyages*, p. 40.

23. Morison, *The Southern Voyages*, p. 42.

24. Columbus, *The Voyage of Christopher Columbus*, p. 85.

25. Columbus, *The Voyage of Christopher Columbus*, p. 93.

26. Columbus, *The Voyage of Christopher Columbus*, p. 94.

27. Columbus, *The Voyage of Christopher Columbus*, p. 105.

28. Columbus, *The Voyage of Christopher Columbus*, pp. 108, 115.

29. Hale, *The Age of Exploration*, p. 56.

30. Quoted in Hale, *The Age of Exploration*, p. 59.

31. Quoted in Morison, *The Southern Voyages*, p. 155.

32. Quoted in Morison, *The Southern Voyages*, p. 157.

Chapter 3: Spices and Gold: Africa, India, and Asia

33. Penrose, *Travel and Discovery in the Renaissance*, p. 63.

34. Penrose, *Travel and Discovery in the Renaissance*, p. 64.

35. Parry, *The Age of Reconnaissance*, p. 139.

36. Penrose, *Travel and Discovery in the Renaissance*, p. 64.

37. Penrose, *Travel and Discovery in the Renaissance*, p. 66.

38. E. G. Ravenstein, trans. and ed., *A Journal of the First Voyage of Vasco da Gama, 1497–1499*. New York: Burt Franklin, 1898, pp. 15, 16.

39. Ravenstein, *A Journal of the First Voyage of Vasco da Gama*, p. 20.

40. Ravenstein, *A Journal of the First Voyage of Vasco da Gama*, pp. 23, 24.

41. Ravenstein, *A Journal of the First Voyage of Vasco da Gama*, p. 42.

42. Ravenstein, *A Journal of the First Voyage of Vasco da Gama*, p. 46.

43. Ravenstein, *A Journal of the First Voyage of Vasco da Gama*, p. 47.

44. Ravenstein, *A Journal of the First Voyage of Vasco da Gama*, p. 55.

45. Ravenstein, *A Journal of the First Voyage of Vasco da Gama*, p. 69.

46. Ravenstein, *A Journal of the First Voyage of Vasco da Gama*, p. 92.

47. Quoted in Hale, *The Age of Exploration*, p. 38.

48. Hale, *The Age of Exploration*, p. 38.

49. Penrose, *Travel and Discovery in the Renaissance*, p. 74.

50. Penrose, *Travel and Discovery in the Renaissance*, p. 75.

51. Parry, *The Age of Reconnaissance*, p. 145.

Chapter 4: Cartographers and Conquistadores: The Exploration of South and Central America

52. Penrose, *Travel and Discovery in the Renaissance*, p. 118.

53. Morison, *The Southern Voyages*, p. 185.

54. Morison, *The Southern Voyages*, p. 186.

55. Quoted in Morison, *The Southern Voyages*, p. 187.

56. Quoted in Morison, *The Southern Voyages*, p. 193.

57. Quoted in Morison, *The Southern Voyages*, p. 203.

58. Morison, *The Southern Voyages*, p. 204.

59. Parry, *The Age of Reconnaissance*, p. 157.

60. Quoted in Morison, *The Southern Voyages*, p. 289.

61. Bernal Díaz, *The Bernal Díaz Chronicles: The True Story of the Conquest of Mexico*. Translated and edited by Albert Idell. New York: Doubleday, 1957, pp. 134, 139–40.

62. Díaz, *The Bernal Díaz Chronicles*, p. 142.

63. Díaz, *The Bernal Díaz Chronicles*, p. 248.

64. Gregory Cerio, "The Black Legend: Were the Spanish That Cruel?" *Newsweek*, Special Issue, October 1992, p. 50.

65. Bill M. Donovan, "Introduction," in Bartolomé de Las Casas, *The Devastation of the Indies: A Brief Account*. Baltimore: Johns Hopkins University Press, 1992, p. 4.

66. de Las Casas, *The Devastation of the Indies*, p. 28.

67. Quoted in Cerio, "The Black Legend," p. 51.

Chapter 5: The First Circumnavigation: Ferdinand Magellan and Juan Sebastián del Cano

68. Bartolomé de Las Casas, *Witness: The Writings of Bartolomé de Las Casas*. Edited and translated by George Sanderlin. Maryknoll, NY: Orbis Books, 1971, 1992, p. 55.

69. Penrose, *Travel and Discovery in the Renaissance*, p. 195.

70. Quoted in Charles E. Nowell, ed. *Magellan's Voyage Around the World: Three Contemporary Accounts by Antonio Pigafetta, Maximilian of Transylvania and Gaspar Correa*. Evanston, IL: Northwestern University Press, 1962, p. 91.

71. Quoted in Nowell, *Magellan's Voyage Around the World*, p. 113.

72. Quoted in Nowell, *Magellan's Voyage Around the World*, p. 109.

73. Quoted in Nowell, *Magellan's Voyage Around the World*, p. 122.

74. Penrose, *Travel and Discovery in the Renaissance*, p. 197.

75. Morison, *The Southern Voyages*, p. 407.

76. Quoted in Nowell, *Magellan's Voyage Around the World*, pp. 123, 128.

77. Quoted in Nowell, *Magellan's Voyage Around the World*, p. 129.

78. Quoted in Nowell, *Magellan's Voyage Around the World*, p. 132.

79. Quoted in Nowell, *Magellan's Voyage Around the World*, p. 136.

80. Quoted in Nowell, *Magellan's Voyage Around the World*, p. 152.

81. Quoted in Nowell, *Magellan's Voyage Around the World*, p. 158.

82. Quoted in Nowell, *Magellan's Voyage Around the World*, pp. 169, 171.

83. Quoted in Nowell, *Magellan's Voyage Around the World*, p. 200.

84. Quoted in Nowell, *Magellan's Voyage Around the World*, p. 255.

85. Quoted in Nowell, *Magellan's Voyage Around the World*, p. 256.

86. Penrose, *Travel and Discovery in the Renaissance*, p. 203.

Chapter 6: The Exploration of North America

87. Samuel Eliot Morison, *The European Discovery of America: The Northern Voyages, A.D. 500–1600*. New York: Oxford University Press, 1971, p. 61.

88. Quoted in Morison, *The Northern Voyages*, p. 159.

89. Quoted in Morison, *The Northern Voyages*, p. 159.

90. Morison, *The Northern Voyages*, p. 187.

91. Quoted in Morison, *The Northern Voyages*, p. 190.

92. Quoted in Morison, *The Northern Voyages*, p. 191.

93. Quoted in Morison, *The Northern Voyages*, p. 211.

94. Morison, *The Northern Voyages*, p. 212.

95. Quoted in Morison, *The Northern Voyages*, p. 212.

96. Morison, *The Northern Voyages*, p. 220.

97. Quoted in Morison, *The Northern Voyages*, p. 213.

98. Quoted in Morison, *The Northern Voyages*, p. 231.

99. Quoted in Morison, *The Northern Voyages*, p. 235.

100. Quoted in Morison, *The Northern Voyages*, p. 287.

101. Quoted in Morison, *The Northern Voyages*, p. 183.

102. Penrose, *Travel and Discovery in the Renaissance*, p. 186.

103. Penrose, *Travel and Discovery in the Renaissance*, p. 186.

104. Quoted in Penrose, *Travel and Discovery in the Renaissance*, p. 191.

Chapter 7: Later Explorations

105. Quoted in Morison, *The Southern Voyages*, p. 622.

106. Morison, *The Southern Voyages*, p. 624.

107. Morison, *The Southern Voyages*, p. 638.

108. Quoted in Morison, *The Southern Voyages*, pp. 628, 629.

109. Morison, *The Southern Voyages*, p. 630.

110. Penrose, *Travel and Discovery in the Renaissance*, p. 153.

111. Quoted in Morison, *The Southern Voyages*, p. 546.

112. Morison, *The Southern Voyages*, p. 548.

113. Penrose, *Travel and Discovery in the Renaissance*, p. 153.

114. Morison, *The Southern Voyages*, p. 554.

115. Hale, *The Age of Exploration*, p. 138.

116. Penrose, *Travel and Discovery in the Renaissance*, p. 226.

117. Penrose, *Travel and Discovery in the Renaissance,* p. 230.

118. Morison, *The Southern Voyages,* p. 651.

119. George Sanderlin, *The Sea-Dragon: Journals of Francis Drake's Voyage Around the World.* New York: Harper & Row, 1969, p. 181.

120. Penrose, *Travel and Discovery in the Renaissance,* p. 233.

Epilogue: A New World

121. Boorstin, *The Discoverers,* p. 185.

122. Boorstin, *The Discoverers,* pp. 192, 201.

123. Jared Diamond, *Guns, Germs and Steel: The Fates of Human Societies.* New York: W. W. Norton, 1997, p. 360.

124. Diamond, *Guns, Germs and Steel,* p. 211.

125. Diamond, *Guns, Germs and Steel,* p. 213.

126. "The Origin of Syphilis," *Discover Magazine,* October 1996, p. 23.

127. Raymond Sokolov, *Why We Eat What We Eat: How the Encounter Between the New World and the Old Changed the Way Everyone on the Planet Eats.* New York: Summit Books, 1991, p. 13.

128. Diamond, *Guns, Germs and Steel,* p. 356.

For Further Reading

Maureen Ash, *Vasco Nunez de Balboa*. Chicago: Childrens Press, 1990. The dramatic story of Balboa's life and exploits in Panama. Good illustrations.

Tony Coulter, *Jacques Cartier, Samuel de Champlain and the Explorers of Canada*. New York: Chelsea House, 1993. A brief account of the exploration of North America by the French.

Jean Fritz, *Around the World in a Hundred Years: From Henry the Navigator to Magellan*. New York: Putnam's, 1994. A good, readable account of the early explorers, by a prominent children's author.

Jean Fritz et al., *The World in 1492*. New York: Henry Holt, 1992. Six noted children's authors discuss what life was like in different parts of the world in 1492. An excellent introduction to the period.

John R. Hale and the editors of Time-Life Books, *The Age of Exploration*. New York: Time, Inc., 1966. A concise and readable account of the period.

Jim Hargrove, *Ferdinand Magellan*. Chicago: Childrens Press, 1990. This book contains many illustrations and makes good use of primary source material, such as Pigafetta's journal.

Stephen R. Lilley, *The Conquest of Mexico*. San Diego: Lucent Books, 1997. Using primary sources from Cortés and his followers, this book presents a thorough account of the European takeover of the Aztec Empire.

Albert Marrin, *The Sea King: Francis Drake and His Times*. New York: Atheneum, 1995. This exciting illustrated biography gives a good picture of Drake, Elizabethan times, and the seafaring life of the sixteenth century.

Milton Meltzer, *Columbus and the World Around Him*. New York: Franklin Watts, 1990. A fine book that puts Columbus in historical perspective.

Rebecca Stefoff, *Vasco da Gama and the Portuguese Explorers*. New York: Chelsea House Publishers, 1993. A readable introduction to the Portuguese enterprise that makes good use of primary sources.

Ronald Syme, *Francisco Coronado and the Seven Cities of Gold*. New York: William Morrow and Company, 1965. Syme uses the journal of one of Coronado's men to bring to life this tale of adventure and discovery.

Works Consulted

Silvio A. Bedini, ed., *The Christopher Columbus Encyclopedia.* New York: Simon & Schuster, 1992. This two-volume set, published to coincide with the five hundredth anniversary of Columbus's first voyage, contains a wealth of information not only about Columbus, but also about the entire age of exploration. The articles are short and readable, and each is signed by a scholar on the subject matter.

Daniel J. Boorstin, *The Discoverers.* New York: Vintage Books, 1985. Boorstin takes a global perspective in this analysis of discoverers through the ages.

Gregory Cerio, "The Black Legend: Were the Spanish That Cruel?" *Newsweek,* Special Issue, October 1992.

Christopher Columbus, *The Voyage of Christopher Columbus: Columbus's Own Journal of Discovery.* Newly restored and translated by John Cummins. New York: St. Martin's Press, 1992.

Hernán Cortés, *Letters from Mexico.* Translated and edited by A. R. Pagden. New York: Orion Press, 1971. These letters from Cortés to supporters in Spain are a crucial primary source of the conquest of Mexico.

Bartolomé de Las Casas, *The Devastation of the Indies: A Brief Account.* Translated from the Spanish by Herma Briffault; introduction by Bill M. Donovan. Baltimore: Johns Hopkins University Press, 1992. This account, first written in 1541 and first published in 1552, is a blistering attack on the Spanish treatment of the American Indians in Central and South America.

————, *Witness: The Writings of Bartolomé de Las Casas.* Edited and translated by George Sanderlin. Maryknoll, NY: Orbis Books, 1971, 1992. This collection of de Las Casas's writings is invaluable in understanding at least one point of view from the sixteenth century.

Jared Diamond, *Guns, Germs and Steel: The Fates of Human Societies.* New York: W. W. Norton, 1997. This Pulitzer Prize–winning book explores the question of why some societies "discover" and conquer others.

Bernal Díaz, *The Bernal Díaz Chronicles: The True Story of the Conquest of Mexico.* Translated and edited by Albert Idell. New York: Doubleday, 1957. This first-person account by one of Cortés's soldiers is clear, complete, and a fascinating look at the Aztec civilization from the Spanish perspective.

Gomes Eannes de Azurara, *The Chronicle of the Discovery and Conquest of Guinea.* Translated into English by Charles Raymond Beazley and Edgar Prestage. Vols. 1 & 2. New York: Burt Franklin, 1896, 1899. Sometimes called Zurara, this contemporary of Prince Henry the Navigator recorded the events of the early voyages to the west coast of Africa.

Robert Kirsch and William S. Murphy, *West of the West: Witnesses to the California Experience, 1542–1906.* New York: E. P. Dutton, 1967. A collection of primary source accounts of California's early days.

John Mandeville, *The Travels of Sir John Mandeville.* New York: Dover Publications, 1964. This is the classic "traveler's tale" of the fourteenth century that encouraged many to explore beyond the known confines of the world.

Samuel Eliot Morison, *The European Discovery of America: The Northern Voyages*, A.D. *500–1600*. New York: Oxford University Press, 1971. Morison is a Columbus scholar and a sailor who actually recreated most of the voyages he recounts in this book and the next. His knowledge of sailing and of the regions discussed makes these two volumes invaluable for anyone interested in the period.

————, *The European Discovery of America: The Southern Voyages*, A.D. *1492–1616*. New York: Oxford University Press, 1974. See note above.

Charles E. Nowell, ed. *Magellan's Voyage Around the World: Three Contemporary Accounts by Antonio Pigafetta, Maximilian of Transylvania and Gaspar Correa*. Evanston, IL: Northwestern University Press, 1962. This useful volume includes the texts of the three surviving contemporary accounts of Magellan's voyage.

J. H. Parry, *The Age of Reconnaissance*. Berkeley: University of California Press, 1963, 1981. Parry gives a thorough account of the shipbuilding, mapmaking, and navigation of the age of exploration.

Boies Penrose, *Travel and Discovery in the Renaissance, 1420–1620*. New York: Atheneum, 1962. This classic work on the age of exploration is a lively, thorough, and highly entertaining history.

Marco Polo, *The Travels of Marco Polo*, a modern translation by Teresa Waugh from the Italian by Maria Bellonci. New York: Facts On File, 1984. Marco Polo's tales of China and Japan encouraged Columbus and many others to attempt to sail there. It is a classic of the fourteenth century, and this translation is readable and entertaining.

E. G. Ravenstein, trans. and ed., *A Journal of the First Voyage of Vasco da Gama, 1497–1499*. New York: Burt Franklin, 1898. The author of this account is unknown, but it is a fascinating firsthand tale of a memorable voyage.

George Sanderlin, *The Sea-Dragon: Journals of Francis Drake's Voyage Around the World*. New York: Harper & Row, 1969. These accounts of the 1577–1580 voyage are spotty in places but provide us with a valuable primary source.

Raymond Sokolov, *Why We Eat What We Eat: How the Encounter Between the New World and the Old Changed the Way Everyone on the Planet Eats*. New York: Summit Books, 1991. A fascinating and entertaining history of food that focuses on the changes that came about in the sixteenth century as a result of the voyages of exploration.

Lawrence C. Wroth, *The Voyages of Giovanni da Verrazzano, 1524–1528*. New Haven, CT: Yale University Press, 1970. A valuable contemporary account of Verrazano's voyage along the coast of North America.

Index

profit motive
  France and, 83
  Portugal and, 21, 25, 47,
    48, 49–50
  as reason for explorations,
    11, 19, 20, 51
  Spain and, 30, 75, 78
Ptolemy, 14–15, 29
Pytheas, 13

Quesada, Gaspar de, 67, 68

raza, la (mestizos), 65
Rey Blanco, El (the White
  King), 94, 95
Rio de la Plata, 92–96
Roberval, Sieur de, 88, 90
Rut, John, 82

sailors, 32, 44
  diet of, 69, 73, 76
  diseases of, 21, 43, 46, 70
Saint Lawrence River, 88
San Antonio (ship), 67, 69
San Salvador, 33
Santa María (ship), 32, 34
Santiago (ship), 67
São Gabriel (ship), 41, 47
São Raphael (ship), 41
scurvy, 21, 43, 46, 70
Serrano, Juan Rodriguez de,
  67, 74
Seven Cities of Cíbola, 85, 86,
  87, 91
ships, 20–21
  see also specific ships
silks, 83
silver, 59–60, 62, 95
Sintra, Pedro de, 24
slaves
  African, 24, 28
  cash crops and, 105
  France and, 86
  native American, 52, 53,
    54, 62–65
  Spain and, 63–65
smallpox, 61, 62, 86
Sokolov, Raymond, 104, 105

Solís, Juan Díaz de, 93
Soto, Hernán de, 55, 85–86,
  87
South Sea. *See* Pacific Ocean
Spain
  explorations by
    of Brazil, 51, 82, 92–95
    of Central America,
      54–55, 57
    circumnavigation of
      globe and, 66–77
    of Colombia, 53–54
    of Mexico, 58–61, 91
    of North America,
      84–87, 91
    of Peru, 61–62
    of Rio de la Plata, 92–96
    of Venezuela, 38, 52
    of West Indies, 30–35,
      36, 37–39, 51–52
  slavery and, 63–65
  Treaty of Tordesillas and,
    36, 38, 66
Spanish Main, 52
Spice Islands, 66, 74–75, 78
spices, 50
  France and, 83
  Portugal and, 76
  Spain and, 75, 78
syphilis, 104

Tainos, 34, 36, 51, 52, 53
Tasman, Abel, 100
Tasmania, 100
Tenochtitlán, 57–61
Terra Incognita, 11, 96, 100
Tlaxcalans, 58, 61, 65
tobacco, 35, 104, 105
Tordesillas, Treaty of, 36, 38,
  48, 66, 81
*Travel and Discovery in the
  Renaissance* (Penrose), 97
Travels of Marco Polo, The
  (Polo), 20
*Travels of Sir John Mandeville,
  The* (Mandeville), 16–17,
  18
Triana, Rodrigo de, 33

Trinidad, 38
Trinidad (ship), 67, 69,
  74–75, 76, 77, 78

Ulloa, Francisco de, 91
Urdaneta, Andrés de, 78

Velázquez, Diego, 58
Venetian Republic, 49
Venezuela, 38, 52
Vergil, Polydore, 81
Verrazano, Giovanni da,
  83–84, 85, 86
Vespucci, Amerigo, 51, 56–57
Victoria (ship), 67, 69, 74–75,
  76, 78
Villiers, Alan, 70
Vinland, 79
*Voyage of Christopher Columbus:
  Columbus's Own Journal of
  Discovery, The* (Columbus),
  33, 34

Waldseemüller, Martin, 56,
  57
Watling Island, 33
weather, 40
West Indies, 57
  Columbus and, 33–35, 36,
    38–39
  Ojeda and, 51, 52
White King, The, 94, 95
Why We Eat What We Eat
  (Sokolov), 105
Windward Islands, 36–37
*Witness: The Writings of
  Bartolomé de Las Casas* (Las
  Casas), 37, 64, 67
writing, 102

Yung-lo (emperor of China),
  102

Zurara, Gomes Eanes de
  on reasons for exploration,
    25
  on sailors' fear of Cape
    Bojador, 23

Picture Credits

Cover photo: Peter Newark's American Pictures

Archive Photos, 25, 32, 48, 52, 54, 75, 78, 83, 84, 87, 89, 102

Corbis-Bettmann, 21, 22, 43, 72, 100, 105

Giraudon/Art Resource, NY, 90

Lambert/Archive Photos, 11

Library of Congress, 28, 29, 31, 35, 36, 37, 42, 55, 56, 65, 68, 70, 80, 81, 97, 107

Lineworks, Inc., 26, 39, 49, 63, 77, 88, 94

North Wind Picture Archives, 17, 47, 60, 61, 62, 103

Prints Old & Rare, 16, 57, 95

Stock Montage, Inc., 10, 14, 41, 45, 49, 76, 98

Baldwin H. Ward/Corbis-Bettmann, 93

About the Author

Sarah Flowers is a writer and a librarian. She holds a B.A. degree in history from Kansas State University; an M.A. degree in history from the University of California, Berkeley; and an M.L.S. from San Jose State University. She loves history and writing for young people. This is her second book in the World History series. She is a librarian for the Santa Clara County Library, in Morgan Hill, California, where she lives with her husband and three sons.

INDEPENDENCE HIGH SCHOOL LIBRARY